FINANCIAL

Dignity ®

after

DIVORCE

A Woman's Guide to Healing
Her Relationship with Money

PRAISE FOR *FINANCIAL DIGNITY*® *AFTER DIVORCE*

"This book will be a game changer for so many women. Christine Luken lays out a clear roadmap to guide, educate, and financially empower women. This is a book every woman should read, regardless of their relationship status, because it is saturated with valuable information that most women are never told. A powerful and eye-opening read!"

— Allison K. Dagney,
Author of *When Tears Leave Scars*
and Thought Work Coach

"In her new book *Financial Dignity*® *After Divorce*, renowned Financial Coach Christine Luken has written a must-read primer for any woman reclaiming her life and financial autonomy after a breakup. Fearlessly using hard-won lessons from her own ghost of relationships past, as well as inspiring first-hand accounts from real-life women, Luken writes with humor, compassion and practicality in equal measure, suggesting simple questions we can ask ourselves as well as actionable, everyday tips we can use to boost our bank account and our money confidence one baby step at a time…Exploring the fascinating neuroscience behind the decisions we make, Luken encourages us to listen to our secret superpower (spoiler alert: it's our emotions!) and outsmart that all-too-familiar "bank account boogeyman": the fear we all have surrounding money. I'm giving this empowering roadmap to financial freedom to every woman in my life—whether she's starting out or starting over!"

— Kristina Mastrocola,
Senior Editor of *Woman's World*
and *First for Women* magazines

"Christine Luken's candid, heart-centered, and action-oriented approach to providing divorcing women with a roadmap to financial empowerment is a must read. I know I would have benefited from this information during my divorce and highly recommend it to others."

— Lacy Garcia,
Founder & CEO of Willow

"*Financial Dignity*® *After Divorce* is the book I desperately needed when I was divorcing my abusive husband. The practical information is all hugely valuable. But Christine Luken offers something absolutely transformational: a way for you to reset your own relationship with money. Any woman who has been in a relationship where they were made to feel worthless financially or emotionally, this book offers you the tools you need to change that."

— Annie Kaszina Ph.D.,
Narcissistic Abuse Recovery Expert

FINANCIAL *Dignity* ®

after

DIVORCE

A Woman's Guide to Healing Her Relationship with Money

CHRISTINE LUKEN

Financial Dignity® After Divorce: A Woman's Guide to Healing Her Relationship with Money

Dedication

To My Husband, Nick Luken,

I'm forever grateful for your support and encouragement of my financial coaching and author business. Thank you most of all for being my soulmate, my rock, and my true partner.

Table of Contents

Introduction

MY ALMOST DIVORCE

he cop threatened to shoot my dog, and at that moment, I knew I had to leave Jeff.

The pounding on the apartment door woke me up at 3 AM. I shuffled to answer it, dressed in my milk and cookies pajamas, my dog, Bronx, at my heels. I grabbed him by the collar and held him behind me as I cautiously cracked open the front door.

Two county cops stood outside, asking for Jeff. He racked up two DUIs in six months, and failed to report for one of his weekends in jail. Jeff had a warrant out for his arrest. *"Where is he?"*

I lied. I told the cops Jeff worked for his dad in Indianapolis and only visited a few times a month. The truth? I had no clue which bar he went to that night, driving a car registered to me, with a suspended license.

The cops asked to search the apartment for him, thinking Jeff might be hiding in a closet or the shower. I complied. Bronx really started barking, with two formidable-looking strangers in our home.

"If you don't control your dog, I'm going to have to shoot him," one of the cops said.

"You're a stranger in MY house, officer, and my dog is doing his job: protecting me. Let me put him in the bathroom until you leave. Don't shoot him, please." I begged.

"Fine."

After a quick sweep of the one-bedroom apartment, the cops departed, and I locked up behind them. I opened the bathroom door, and Bronx bolted out to me. I sank to the floor and sobbed, hugging my dog.

Strangely, although I was rattled, I wasn't mad at the cop. I was pissed as hell at Jeff for putting me in this position. Without his irresponsibility and constant drinking, the cops wouldn't have come in the first place.

I wanted out of this relationship, now. *The problem?* I had no money to leave. I needed support and a plan to get out. I reached out to my Dad for help. He didn't give me or lend me money, but he did give me a safe place to stay while I regrouped and got back on my feet financially.

You might be surprised to learn that I didn't get divorced. But it's only because Jeff and I never got married. Back at the apartment, my gorgeous wedding dress hung unworn in the closet, and a non-refundable deposit secured our reception hall. Although I wanted to sell it, I returned my engagement ring to Jeff because his mother co-signed the loan for it. (And she was crazy, so I didn't want to be in her crosshairs.) Leaving Jeff was difficult, but necessary.

Money took center stage during most of our arguments. Jeff changed jobs the way most people change their socks, and he was no stranger to the unemployment office. His financial irresponsibility and erratic income caused much of the conflict in our relationship.

Our relationship resembled a roller coaster of dysfunction, and money certainly wasn't our only issue. There was the partying, drinking, drug use, lying, and suspected (but never proven) infidelity.

I call it my "almost divorce," because I *almost* got married. But I didn't. And for that I am grateful.

In April 2000, I broke off my seven-year relationship with him. Although never legally married, Jeff and I were financially entangled. Because he had no credit, we racked up all of our debt in my name. Due to his two DUIs, I technically owned his car and insured it. Jeff and I rented an apartment together with both of our names on the lease. We were pet parents to our dog, Bronx, and two cats, Yin Yang and Precious. We owned furniture and a myriad of other things together.

When I told Jeff our relationship was over, financial loose ends still needed to be taken care of and tied up. Seeing him after the breakup felt worse than the breakup itself. I remember leaving those encounters—signing over the car title so he could sell it to his friend, retrieving my things from our apartment (after three weeks he already had another woman moved in)—feeling furious and distraught.

At 26 years old, I hit financial rock-bottom, despite having my accounting degree and working as the accounting manager for my father's company. I experienced a crushing sense of shame and embarrassment. I owed three payday lenders money. I was two months behind on my car payment. I think my credit score might have been negative, if that's possible. I had no money to rent another apartment when I broke up with Jeff, so I moved into the spare bedroom at my dad's house. The good thing about hitting rock bottom is there's nowhere else to go but up.

I had a choice to make when the money shame overwhelmed me: would I hide from it, or choose to get help so I could break the cycle? Thankfully, I was smart enough to know that I needed therapy after my "almost divorce." I had no idea what a healthy relationship looked like, and I didn't want to repeat the past. My counselor, Dave, gave a name to my dysfunction: codependency.

Jeff and I had an unhealthy parent/child dynamic in our relationship, which is the essence of codependency. He required constant bailing out, both literally and figuratively. Jeff got into trouble, financial or otherwise, and I would swoop in to rescue him. Needless to say, it caused a great deal of strife and tension. I felt resentment for having to carry all of the load financially in the relationship.

A third "person" existed in our relationship: Money. Money got caught in the crossfire of negativity on a regular basis. Money was constantly pulled into the center of our scream-fests. Although my relationship with Jeff was beyond fixing, I needed to successfully repair my relationship with money. Why? Because money and I will be together forever, and the same is true for you.

Fortunately, I got the help and healing I needed. I put in the work, both on my mindset and the practical changes in my finances. After many ups and downs, my story has a happy ending. I've used my negative experiences and hard lessons to teach and coach countless women to heal their relationships with money, too.

Whether you're leaving a long-term relationship or going through a divorce, this book will guide you to a place of lasting Financial Dignity®. I've experienced many of the same feelings and situations as you, and I want to give you hope. You can recover a positive and peaceful relationship with your money, and I'm going to show you how. I'll guide you down the path, but you have to do the walking. It might not always be easy, but I promise, it will be worth it!

Here's how to make the most of this book. Go to www.FinancialDignityAfterDivorce.com to download the companion workbook. There are questions to consider and action items at the end of most of the chapters. Just reading this book will give you knowledge, but if you apply and integrate what you learn, it will change your life. Commit to yourself right now that you'll fully participate in this process by writing out your answers and doing the exercises. Let's get started!

Part One

Breaking Up is Hard to Do

Chapter 1

THE FINANCIAL FALLOUT
OF YOUR DIVORCE

hether you are divorced, separated, or ending a long-term relationship, there will be financial fallout! It's rare that someone escapes the demise of a long-term relationship financially unscathed. And unfortunately, women tend to take the brunt of it. The stats regarding the impact of divorce on women's income and standard of living vary. On average, a woman's standard of living goes down 27 percent after divorce, while a man's decreases by 10 percent. Some studies on this issue even show that men's standard of living even *increases* after divorce.

One of the reasons your standard of living might decrease is due to taking time away from the workplace to raise children. When you're thrust back into the job market due to necessity, you might feel like a fish out of water. Your job skills from five or ten years ago feel out of date, and you might not be able to immediately go back to a similar position making similar money.

Add to that the simple math of divorce or a breakup. You're dividing your assets in half and doubling your expenses. You and your husband once shared expenses like a house payment, rent, utilities, insurance, and groceries. Now you'll have to cover those 100 percent on your own. Of course, if you have children or there's a sizable income disparity, you may be entitled to receive child support or spousal maintenance for a period of time. But more than likely, you will have to make adjustments to your spending in the short term, while you work on increasing your income.

And of course, there is the cost of the divorce itself. The average cost of a divorce ranges wildly. An uncontested divorce in the Midwest might set you back $5,000 or less, but a contested divorce in Los Angeles or New York City could cost you tens of thousands of dollars. This cost includes attorneys' fees, court costs, and the cost of hiring outside experts like a tax adviser, child custody evaluator, or real estate appraiser.

Because of this reality, there will be hard, and often emotional, decisions to make. Some things that were no-brainer buys for you in the past might not be affordable post-divorce. It's going to feel painful to give up or cut back on cleaning services, manicures, massages, yoga studio memberships, and other self-pampering treats. It's going to be downright excruciating to tell your darling five-year-old she can no longer participate in dance or gymnastics because mommy can't afford it.

If you have assets like home equity, retirement funds, vehicles, and bank balances to divide up, consider yourself lucky. For many women, divorce and bankruptcy go hand in hand, especially when all you're fighting over is the debt.

Unfortunately, my mother-in-law, Jackie (who's now in heaven, rest her soul) experienced this back in 2004. Jackie's then-husband, Steve, cheated on her with a woman half her age. As a couple, they always lived on the edge of broke, so the only thing divided between them in divorce court was the debt. Steve remained living in their house and was supposed to be making the mortgage payment.

Several months later, Steve filed for bankruptcy and shortly after that, the house went into foreclosure. Because Jackie's name remained on the mortgage account, the bank came to her for payment. Her only sources of income were social security and a part-time job. It's rare that I encourage anyone to file bankruptcy, but in Jackie's situation, it truly was the only good solution for her.

I want you to take some time to look at how your income and expenses have changed (or are changing) because of your divorce or breakup. It's important to know exactly what you are dealing with so you can take productive action. Acknowledging and mourning over the financial consequences of divorce is part of the healing process!

QUESTIONS TO CONSIDER:

What role did money play in the ending of your relationship?

Did you and your ex fight about money or not talk about it at all?

How did you and your ex differ in your views and treatment of money?

What money issues were continual sources of stress in your relationship?

What's changed in your finances because of divorce or separation?

What feels harder now? What's new that you now have to deal with?

Chapter 2

Your Divorce & Money Checklist

*H*ere are the practical money moves you should make as soon as the D-word is mentioned by either you or your soon-to-be-ex, in order to financially protect yourself.

Open a PO Box for receiving financial and sensitive correspondence. You can do this at your local post office or a UPS Store. Another option is sending this type of mail to a trusted friend or family member's address. Ruth Jackson, an experienced divorce attorney cautions, "Watch the mail to see what's received from financial institutions. Gather financial documents, make copies of those documents, and provide those copies to a trusted friend or family member to ensure that you have as much information as possible."

Open a new bank account in your name only. This should be at a different bank from your husband's current accounts. If he's friendly with the teller or banking manager, that person might mention the account to him or even tell him the balance, even though his name is not on it.

Start setting aside money for your attorney's fees in your new account. Each of you will have your own divorce lawyer, and most require a deposit to retain them on your behalf.

If you don't have a credit card in your name only, get one. It might be difficult for you to apply for one later, especially if your husband is the primary income source in your household. Now, please understand, I'm not suggesting you run up the balance on this credit card. Having a credit card to use and pay off monthly is a positive influence on your credit score. This will be helpful in the future if you're going to apply for a mortgage or a car loan on your own.

Check your credit report for free at the following site: www.AnnualCreditReport.com. Shelley Funke Frommeyer, a divorced woman, CFP®, and Founder of FFR Wealth, provides a word of warning. She wishes she'd understood the importance of protecting her identity and credit score during her divorce. "Mysteriously, my application for credit at the Honda dealership was denied shortly after my divorce. When the salesman showed me my credit report, I was astounded to discover my ex-husband provided my social security number to lease his pickup truck. He was seven months past due on payments! All of it reflected on my credit report, in addition to two maxed out and past due credit cards! He accrued over $35,000 in debt without me even knowing it!"

Checking your credit report is important because it might reveal debt your husband incurred in your name or jointly that you're unaware of. It will also show the payment history of all loans in your name. If your husband has a gambling or substance abuse problem, excessive use of debt to fund these habits is common. You'll be able to see outstanding balances and if payments have been made on time.

Check your credit score. You might be able to do this for free if you have a credit card with certain banks. If not, there's usually a small fee to check it through various websites.

Make copies of current statements for all jointly held bank accounts, credit cards, loans, investment and retirement accounts, and other household bills. Your attorney will ask for this information, so go ahead and gather it up. You'll also need to reference this information when making your interim budget, to manage your spending while waiting for the divorce to be finalized.

Close joint credit accounts with zero balances. This will remove the temptation for either of you to run up these credit accounts unnecessarily.

Make copies of the last three years' worth of tax returns. Your divorce attorney will also ask for these, so make sure you have them. You can go straight to your CPA's office for copies, if you don't know where your spouse keeps them.

Find a financial planner who is a Certified Divorce Financial Analyst® (CDFA®), especially if you or your husband have significant retirement assets. These financial planners specialize in divorce situations and know the laws governing the division of these types of assets in your state. A CDFA® will also help you properly invest these assets post-divorce as you make plans for your future retirement. If your financial planner isn't a CDFA®, just make sure he or she regularly serves divorcing clients.

Create an interim budget for yourself to ensure financial stability as you go through the divorce process.

ACTION ITEMS:

Visit the website below to download the checklist and start checking things off!

www.FinancialDignityAfterDivorce.com

Chapter 3

WHERE DIVORCING
HUSBANDS HIDE MONEY

athy*, a woman in her early sixties, considered filing for divorce from her alcoholic husband. Friends and family tried several interventions with no success. Despite his boozing, her husband still managed to hold down his high-paying job, but they fought constantly about money. Kathy feared her husband would hide money from her as divorce loomed. She already felt in the dark about their spending, assets, income, and debt. Her fears were confirmed when she found $4,000 of cash in his briefcase, along with deposit slips for an account she didn't know existed.

Is your soon-to-be ex being evasive, secretive, or defensive about financial details as divorce is looming? Could he be hiding something from you? Approximately 37% of people keep at least one financial secret from their romantic partner, so you'd be wise to do a little investigating to make sure. Hiding money goes beyond stuffing cash in a briefcase. Divorcing spouses hide income, cash, valuables, and even debt from their partners.

Where do divorcing husbands hide income? If he works a traditional job, he could be split-depositing his paycheck. Your husband might deposit a set amount into your joint account and deposit part of his regular paycheck, overtime, or bonuses into a separate account in his name only. When I worked in Human Resources years ago, a male employee regularly asked me to deposit his quarterly profit-sharing check into a separate account from his regular paycheck, so his wife wouldn't know about it.

If separation or divorce is looming, your husband might defer a bonus, raise, or promotion. If he knows he's up for an increase in income, your husband might ask his boss to wait until your divorce is final to give him a promotion so your child support or maintenance is based on his current (lower) salary.

Cindy Alisha Gunraj, a Certified Divorce Coach, says, "It's important to find and document as many assets as you can up front, especially if you're dealing with a partner who likes to hide money. My partner tried to hide $200,000 of his pension money from me! It was found in a forensic analysis." If you don't know what types of benefits your soon-to-be ex has through work beyond his salary, it's vital you find out. You could discover he has stock options or pension benefits that you might be entitled to in the division of assets.

Business-owning husbands have even more places to hide income. If your husband owns his own business or professional practice, there are many opportunities to artificially lower income. He could receive client payments in cash, keeping the income "off the books." Your husband might purposely overpay vendors or the IRS, knowing he'll get refunds after the divorce is final. He could also delay the receipt of orders or customer payments. If your husband is a business owner and his once successful venture started having money problems right around the time of divorce, it might be wise to retain a forensic accountant.

Today's divorcing husbands have moved way beyond stashing a roll of cash in their sock drawer. (But you should totally look there, too.) In this digital age where everything is trackable, they're getting creative. Buying prepaid gift cards or getting cash back while shopping with joint money has become a popular way to "hide" cash. Your soon-to-be ex could buy a $50 prepaid Visa card or receive cash back every week at the grocery store and you wouldn't know it by looking at bank or credit card statements. It would just get buried in your monthly food expenses. Meanwhile, he's stashing the cash or gift cards to use later.

You might think it's a wonderful thing for your spouse to open a college savings account in your child's name. However, these accounts are *not* considered marital assets, and therefore you won't get any of this money in the divorce. Yet, as the custodian of the account, your husband has complete control over it and could cash it out (with a penalty) after the divorce, never intending it to be used for college expenses.

Maybe your husband's collection of baseball cards, old motorcycle parts, or comic books is a childish waste of money. Maybe not. In truth, those "hobbies" could really be worth a small fortune. A divorcing husband might ramp up his collecting in order to convert joint cash into an asset he knows you won't fight for. If your husband has an extensive collection of coins, sports memorabilia, firearms, or the like, you can request that it be formally valued for the division of assets.

Linda E Bauer, President and Wealth Manager at Uplevel Financial Services, cautions, "Take great care to document belongings in the household as well as finances before announcing the intent to seek divorce. If not, you might find valuable things disappearing from your house or property, as one of my clients did. Upon announcing her intention to seek an attorney for divorce, she noticed jewelry, art, and other valuables missing from their home. Her husband had leased an apartment to keep the valuables…and also his mistress. It was a mess!"

You've heard of Bitcoin and maybe even Ethereum. But, as I write this chapter, there are over 10,000 different cryptocurrencies divorcing husbands can purchase to hide assets from the divorce court. Cryptocurrency is notoriously hard to find and track, which makes it an enticing place for deceptive spouses to park money. In fact, there's a whole new field of forensic accounting springing up to help divorcing spouses track it down.

Sometimes it's literally hiding cash, valuables, and gift cards in places they don't think you'd ever look. Of course, he might have a trusted friend, family member, or new girlfriend hold cash for him, but sometimes it's right under your nose – or over your head. A prominent divorce attorney in Cincinnati told me the #1 place where husbands hide money is in the drop ceiling! Other common spots include tool boxes, hunting duffle bags, in their desk at the office, gun safes, golf bags, and tackle boxes. If you're in the middle of divorce and you come across cash or other valuables your husband is hiding, document everything. Snap pictures on your phone, and email the evidence to your divorce attorney, which will automatically put a date and time stamp on it.

Sometimes your husband isn't hiding income or cash from you; he's hiding debt. I frequently see this scenario when there is infidelity or a substance abuse issue. Keep a close eye on your joint credit accounts, and monitor your credit report. Divorcing husbands might open new credit cards, request lines of credit, or even take out payday loans. You can freeze current joint credit cards so no new charges can be made, if you think this could be a problem. Red flags include your suddenly not being able to access online account information or paper statements that mysteriously stop coming to the house.

Kim West, divorce coach and Founder of Navigating the Knot says, "I learned that my husband had accrued $30,000 of debt on a credit card he kept secret from me. I never carried a balance on a credit card and had an impeccable credit score, so learning that he had hidden debt and could potentially saddle me with some of it was terrifying."

If he's desperate for cash, your husband can initiate a new loan against his 401(k) account without your knowledge. If you suspect your soon-to-be ex is running up new debt, check your credit report and credit score ASAP. You might also want to put a freeze on your credit until the divorce is over. Just be aware this will also affect your access to new credit during this time. Unfortunately, I've even seen identity theft perpetrated by spouses, where the debt is taken out in your name, not his, without your knowledge or consent. And the only way to resolve it is to file a criminal charge against him!

Bryan Goldstein, a divorce attorney, told me, "I had a case once where my client's husband earned well over one million dollars per year. Unfortunately, the wife had no idea he had a severe gambling issue, among other bad habits. The husband stopped paying their mortgage, racked up a tax liability of over $700,000, plus hundreds of thousands of dollars in credit card debt. Despite their high income and lavish living, this couple was in an incredible amount of debt, and the wife didn't even realize it."

If your husband is "playing dirty" and hiding money, should you do it, too? After all, you want to protect yourself financially, and the best defense is a good offense, right? This is a discussion you need to have with your attorney as soon as you confirm that your husband is hiding income, cash, assets, or debt.

It's a wise idea to open a separate account in your name only as soon as you decide you're filing for divorce. This is to ensure that you have access to cash, not necessarily to hide it. Separate money doesn't mean secret money, and you will need to disclose it to your attorney. Any money you receive as income or gifts can go into this account.

If your husband is abusive or financially controlling, you might not have a choice but to take drastic measures to survive and break his hold on you. I talk to many women who are coming out of such relationships who wanted out much sooner, but didn't file for divorce because they couldn't afford it.

My client, Allison K. Dagney, author of the memoir *When Tears Leave Scars*, told me that hiding money over a period of many months was the only way she could pay her divorce attorney. Her husband worked for a major financial services company and controlled the household money with an iron fist. He restricted Allison's access to the family finances and regularly told her she didn't have the smarts to handle money wisely. The only receipts he didn't scrutinize were grocery related. So, Allison got $25-$50 cash back every time she made a grocery purchase and hid the money until she had saved enough to hire her attorney and file for divorce.

QUESTIONS TO CONSIDER & ACTION ITEMS:

Has your spouse been acting defensive or evasive when you ask about financial matters?

Do a little investigating on your own to be sure he's not hiding income, assets, or debt from you. If you suspect the amounts are significant, consider hiring a forensic accountant.

Chapter 4

COSTLY DIVORCE MISTAKES

There are numerous missteps that can cause you financial damage, but I want to call your attention to three particularly costly divorce mistakes. This is especially important if you're in the thick of the divorce or separation process.

Mistake #1 is using the same divorce lawyer as your soon-to-be ex-spouse. Speaking of divorce attorneys, you should definitely have your own. I've seen situations where a woman is talked into using the same lawyer as her spouse on the premise that it will save money. Be especially wary if your ex is personal friends with the attorney! Even in cases of collaborative divorce, each person has their own counsel.

You need your own legal advisor, one who is representing *your* best interests during the divorce. Do not be bullied into using the same lawyer as your soon-to-be ex. Yes, it will cost you a little more money up front to have your own attorney, but it's almost always worth it in the long run.

Mistake #2 is "playing ostrich." When you ignore dealing with your money issues, you're like the ostrich who buries its head in the sand. You might avoid dealing with your finances because you're overwhelmed mentally and emotionally. Plus, if the divorce isn't final yet, it feels like you're chasing a moving target. How can you create a plan if you don't know what your "new normal" even looks like?

However, avoidance of your personal finances can have unpleasant results. If you ignore bills or pay them late, the consequences might include higher interest rates, late fees, or a lower credit score. This is the last thing you need right now!

If you were relatively uninvolved with the money management before your divorce, taking charge of it by yourself can feel like a daunting task. Women in this situation have told me they feel ashamed or stupid that they couldn't figure it out on their own.

Although facing your finances head-on seems scary, it's the only way to take control and start moving in a better direction. Become a sponge and absorb as much good information on money management as you can, especially the areas that are hard or confusing for you. My book *Money Is Emotional: Prevent Your Heart from Hijacking Your Wallet* walks you through both the emotional and practical sides of all areas of personal finance. It's a great place to start. If you want additional guidance, I highly recommend seeking out a money coach, CPA, or financial advisor to teach you the basics. You could even ask a money-smart friend or family member to help you comb through the numbers and set up your spending plan.

When you earn a six-figure income, receive spousal support, or have a significant lump sum settlement, it's easier to play ostrich. When money is tight, you are forced to deal with it and manage it wisely, so you can meet your needs. But when there's more than enough to pay the bills every month, you don't have to watch the details as closely. And that can actually be a bad thing.

Here's why: When your support stops or the settlement dwindles down too fast, it's going to be a tough reality check.

You'd be wise to dig into the numbers and proactively manage your money when there's more than enough. This will help you to save, invest, and pay off debt, so you're in a solid position when the child support and maintenance runs out. I've had women call me in a panic a year before their support stops because they never planned what to do when the cut in income arrives, even though they knew it was coming for ten years.

If you are going through an especially messy divorce that includes custody battles, restraining orders, and lawyers fighting over assets, you are in survival mode. You probably don't have the emotional bandwidth to focus on managing your money. It is imperative in this situation to have someone help you. A financial coach will set you up on a personalized plan so all you need to do is follow it. You might even want to hire a daily money manager to pay bills and handle your accounts for you. This will get you through a time of temporary crisis without dropping the ball on your finances.

Mistake #3 is not having a third-party sounding board. Your friends and family mean well. And although they love you, they are not objective. Even if your mom is a CPA or your best friend is a banker, you need someone who is completely unbiased to help you navigate the emotional and financial challenges of divorce.

I recommend consulting with a financial coach, CPA, or financial planner (particularly a CDFA®, Certified Divorce Financial Analyst®) to assist you in the money arena. Why? These experts will look at your entire financial picture and create a plan to carry you into your future. But you don't just need help with the practical money issues. In addition, I highly recommend individual counseling with a therapist who specializes in divorce.

You might be eligible to receive free counseling through your workplace's Employee Assistance Program. You can contact your HR representative to see if you have this benefit. And if you're still legally married, you can access this benefit via your husband's employer, if you're not working a traditional job. If you're unable to afford therapy, another option is a divorce support group. Getting the support you need can prevent you from making emotional money mistakes you'll regret later.

QUESTIONS TO CONSIDER & ACTION ITEMS:

Are you burying your head in the sand when it comes to managing your money?

Is there one particular area, such as retirement or life insurance, that you're avoiding?

Who do you have as an objective, yet supportive, third party who can help you with emotional money decisions? If you don't have someone, ask around for recommendations!

Chapter 5

SHOULD I STAY OR SHOULD I GO?

I'm not talking about your relationship. I'm talking about your home. Should you stay or should you go? Many women want to stay in their current house for the sake of their children. Divorce is a traumatic change for any family, no matter the age of your kids. Moms can feel guilty even considering adding more changes like selling the house and moving, especially if it involves their child changing schools.

Women have said to me, "I don't care what it costs to keep the house. I want to do this for my kids, so I'll figure out how to make it work." But what if the numbers don't work? The best gift you can give your children is to be a calm, confident, and financially strong parent. If you are spending down assets or racking up debt trying to stay in a house you can't truly afford, you're going to be a stressed-out emotional wreck. Sometimes it's you who feels emotionally attached to your current home, and that's understandable. Just remember that you can make any house, apartment, or condo feel like home. "Home" is a feeling, not a location!

If you stay in your marital home, the courts usually dictate that you pay your ex-spouse 50% of the home's equity. This involves refinancing the home and having the mortgage liability in your name only, plus removing your spouse's name from the property deed. At closing, your ex will be paid out his share of the equity so he can purchase or rent another house.

If your ex is keeping the house, the reverse happens. He refinances the house into his name, paying you out your share of the equity, and removing your name from the deed. If neither of you wants to remain in your marital home, the house is sold and the equity, after Realtor's fees and closing costs, is split 50/50.

Sounds pretty cut and dry right? Unfortunately, things don't always go smoothly in this process. What if the person who wants to stay in the home isn't able to qualify for financing? What if you thought your name was taken off the mortgage, but, oops, it wasn't? What if major repairs are needed on the house before it can be sold to anyone?

As great as home ownership can be, if it's not done right, it can be more of a curse than a blessing. Women tend to underestimate the additional costs of being a homeowner versus a renter. When you're renting, your landlord pays for the taxes, maintenance, and emergency breakdowns. If you're a homeowner, that's all on you. Plus, you'll either have to hire someone or do all the yard and home maintenance yourself. If you don't have a savings account to take care of fixing or replacing major appliances and other upkeep, home ownership is going to stress you out to the max!

Since your life is in transition, purchasing real estate might not be the right move for you at this time. If you just got divorced, renting an apartment, house, or condo could be the best solution for now. The problem with buying and selling a home is that the process takes time and money. If a newly divorced woman buys a house, then decides a year later to move to another state to be closer to her grown children, she's going to have to deal with the expense and stress of selling a house on top of moving. Renting for a year or two while you heal from divorce and figure out your future plans might save you both money and effort.

The other thing to consider is that home ownership ties you to a specific location. While many women love this fact, there are others who feel stifled by this. If you're child-free (or your kids are grown) and you love to travel, buying a house or condo might not be the best choice for you. Maybe you'd rather spend your time and money exploring the world. If you own a home and travel extensively for work or pleasure, you'll end up paying someone to care for your property while you're away. Renting a place might be a much better option for those happily afflicted with wanderlust.

"Should I stay or should I go?" As you can see, the answer to that question is "It depends." Whether you're buying or selling a house, you definitely want to hire an experienced real estate professional. If you and your spouse decide to sell the house, look for a real estate professional who is a Certified Divorce Specialist or has a niche for helping divorcing couples.

QUESTIONS TO CONSIDER:

Will you stay in your current home?

Can you reasonably afford to do so?

Are you feeling guilty about moving your kids to another house or school?

Are you feeling sad about leaving your current home? It's okay to grieve the loss of your house, especially if you really love it and have good memories there.

Chapter 6

UNDERSTANDING THE STAGES OF GRIEF

*D*ivorce involves loss on multiple levels. Yes, you are losing your relationship with your spouse. You might also be losing the home you lived in during your marriage. If you have kids, you will lose the time they are spending with your ex. And of course, you're likely going to come out of the divorce with fewer financial resources.

Divorce is essentially the death of your marriage, and you will likely experience some or all of the stages of grief. This is a normal part of the healing process. You might go through some or all of the stages of grief in any order. You can return to the various stages, depending on what you're experiencing. The stages of grief affect your emotional well-being, and potentially your financial behavior, so it's important to be aware of them.

It's not uncommon to experience multiple losses in divorce scenarios. Several years ago, Maria* hired me to help her navigate her finances during her divorce. She owned and operated a business with her husband, Ted. He initiated the divorce because he was in love with a female employee who worked for the business. Ted decided he wanted to keep the family home and buy Maria out of the business. So my client dealt simultaneously with three losses: the loss of her home, the loss of her job (including her friends and support system there), and the loss of her marriage. I helped Maria identify the stages of grief and showed her how to navigate her money decisions as she moved through them.

Here are the five stages of grief, known as the Kubler-Ross model of grief.

Denial: In this stage, you're experiencing shock, like the divorce situation isn't real. "I can't believe this is happening" is your dominant thought. You might be in shock that your spouse wants a divorce, or you might be surprised by your own admission that you want out of the marriage.

Most people move through the denial stage in a matter of days or weeks. A woman in denial might refuse to accept the fact that the divorce is happening. She might say, "I don't think he's serious. He's going to change his mind."

The danger comes in getting stuck in the denial stage for an extended period. There are important legal and financial tasks to take care of at the beginning of the divorce process (see the Divorce and Money Checklist in Chapter 2.) Denial can keep us from taking proactive and positive action with our money.

Anger: Anytime there is a loss in our lives, we can experience anger. You could feel anger toward your ex, the other woman, with yourself, and even with God / the Universe. Your dominant thoughts are "Why is this happening to me? This isn't fair! I'm so mad at him!"

Anger is a normal response when we feel someone has wronged us. You might be completely justified in your anger, as my client Maria was when she found out her husband was cheating on her. She didn't initiate the divorce. She didn't want to move from the home she lived in for 18 years. She didn't want to leave the employees of their business who were like family to her.

You can argue that the situation is unfair and blame others. If you're in victim mode, you're not owning your power over the situation. No, you can't change the past or control what others do or say to you. But you can control your response to it. Do not make major financial decisions in the heat of anger! Let your emotions subside, and then decide. Physical activities like running, yoga, swimming, kickboxing, or hiking are constructive outlets for angry energy.

Bargaining or Negotiating: The unhealthy version of this stage of grief is characterized by trying to change or delay the loss of the marriage. A woman might try to bargain with or convince her spouse to return after a separation or breakup, even if there is an unhealthy dynamic in a relationship.

There is also a healthier side to this stage of grief, and that is entering into the negotiating process, with the aid of your attorney, to settle the details of the divorce. When it comes to money, you need to ask yourself, "Am I negotiating from a place of desperation or of level-headed calm?"

Depression: In this stage of grief, you recognize and mourn your losses. You feel sad, spend time crying and grieving, and might isolate yourself for a period of time. It's normal to feel sadness over the loss of your marriage, even if you are the one initiating the divorce.

Please note that this is not necessarily clinical depression. Clinical depression is marked by a depressed mood most of the day, and a loss of interest in normal activities and relationships, with symptoms that are present every day for at least two weeks.

If you're in this stage of grief, beware of emotional spending as a way to self-soothe. I'm a firm believer in having some money earmarked for self-care in your spending plan. Investing in a massage, yoga classes, or even a mani-pedi is a better way to cheer yourself up while taking care of yourself. Spending money on random stuff usually doesn't have the same return.

Acceptance: You accept your loss. You understand the divorce situation logically and have come to terms with it emotionally. You are prepared to deal with the legal and financial tasks necessary to move forward with your life.

It's important to have grace with yourself as you move through the stages of grief. You're probably going to get sick of me saying this, but...a counselor or therapist will assist you in processing these emotions in a healthy and productive way. Trying to ignore them or "stuff them" only prolongs your suffering.

QUESTIONS TO CONSIDER:

What stage of grief are you currently experiencing?
What can you do to take care of yourself during this time?

Chapter 7

YOUR DIVORCE MONEY TEAM

ou will be making numerous financial decisions both during and after your divorce. Some of these decisions can have long-lasting consequences. Major money moves like refinancing debt, buying or selling real estate, purchasing investments, and starting a business are better made with expert guidance. Don't rely solely on your divorce attorney for advice. He or she is an expert in divorce law, not personal finance.

"Plans go wrong for lack of advice; many advisors bring success," said King Solomon, who is considered to be one of the wisest people to ever walk the face of the earth. If he thought it was a good idea to have advisors, maybe *we* ought to pay attention. Who is on your Money Team? We have this idea that only millionaires or billionaires need a Money Team, but you'll need one if you want to achieve lasting Financial Dignity®.

Even if you're a numbers person like me, it's still difficult to be an expert in every area of money. I'm an expert on spending, saving, and debt, but I need the input of qualified experts when it comes to taxes, insurance, and investments. Some of these fields—like tax accounting—are a labyrinth of rules and regulations. You'd be foolish and reckless to try and go it alone.

When selecting people for a spot on your Money Team, ensure they are heart-centered, focused on serving you rather than selling you. Yes, of course, these experts should also have the credentials and experience. "Talk to several people to get a feel for their fit with you," says Melissa Joy, CFP®, CDFA®. "Do they seem competent as well as personable? Would you like to be with them on an emotional journey?" These financial professionals should explain things in a way you can understand, welcome your questions, and never "mansplain" anything to you. Who should be on your Money Team? Here are candidates to consider.

A CPA, Accountant, or other Tax Professional ensures that you are compliant with current tax laws without paying more than necessary. As your financial life becomes fuller and more complex, a good tax professional helps you legally minimize your taxes so you can protect your nest egg. My CPA is a vital part of my Money Team because keeping up with tax law changes is a full-time job. (And I got a D in tax accounting in college, so there's that.)

It's important to retain an **estate planning attorney** immediately after your divorce is final. This attorney will help you draw up a new will and set up trusts, if appropriate for your situation. Ask your divorce attorney for a recommendation. They might have a colleague in their law firm who can handle this for you. Consult with an attorney before entering into business deals, partnerships, leasing agreements, and other contracts. Legal documents are confusing, and if you sign something you don't understand, it could cost you dearly in the long run.

Most of us hate paying our insurance premiums every month, but these policies protect us against catastrophic financial blows. **Your insurance agent** helps you navigate the various choices for coverage to ensure your risks are covered. It's wise to talk with several insurance agents, gather information, and compare prices so you can make an educated decision on your insurance needs.

If you already have some retirement assets, you definitely need the expertise of a **financial planner or investment advisor**. If you're still in the divorce process, I highly recommend finding a professional who is a CDFA®, a Certified Divorce Financial Analyst. A CDFA® understands the appropriate division and evaluation of retirement assets in divorce cases. Their recommendations are frequently submitted in divorce cases for judges to consider. A CDFA® is also comfortable appearing in court and testifying on your behalf. (If your divorce is already behind you, having a financial planner with this designation isn't as important.)

Depending on your personal situation, there might be additional players you want on your Money Team. If you're struggling with your spending and debt reduction plan, enlist the help of a **financial coach**. Find one who's a Certified Divorce Specialist®, or who has experience guiding clients through divorce situations. If you plan on buying a house within the next year or so, connect with a **mortgage broker** or the residential lending officer at your bank. They will help you get your financial ducks in a row so the mortgage process goes smoothly when you're ready to buy. I would also interview two or more **Realtors®** several months before putting your house on the market. This is one of the biggest financial transactions you may make in your lifetime, and you want a professional real estate agent to handle it, not your cousin Ashley who recently just passed the test for her real estate license! If you have kids in middle or high school, connecting with a **college planning expert** is an excellent idea.

A money-smart and responsible friend or family member should be on your Money Team. This person knows your strengths and weaknesses. He or she should be able to give you honest feedback and help you uncover your blind spots. You're not necessarily asking for this person's specific financial advice, but rather perspective on the situation and your reaction to it. We all need at least one person with whom we can openly discuss our financial details, knowing the conversations will be safe and confidential. This friend or family member might also be a good source of recommendations to potential candidates for open spots on your Money Team.

In general, be cautious of having close friends or family members as paid professionals on your Money Team. I've seen my clients make bad decisions regarding insurance policies and investments, because they were sold to them by their best friend or father-in-law. If you're considering this, be sure to get a second or third opinion before bringing this person onto your Money Team. I fired my former financial planner (who was also a friend) and it made things between us awkward for more than two years.

Another word of caution: Don't search for "expert" advice on the cheap. The cost of hiring an amateur to be on your Money Team can be very expensive indeed. However, I don't want you to overpay for expert advice either. "Don't do it alone. Instead of DIY, I suggest the DIT approach (do it together) with a team of professionals looking after every aspect: the legal, emotional, and financial ones," says Holistic Divorce Coach, Olga Nadal.

I recommend you get a second opinion on your insurance policies and investments every few years to ensure you're still receiving solid advice and a fair price. Be certain to meet with the members of your Money Team on a regular basis to stay on track with your financial plan and value their contribution.

If you and your ex still have the same insurance agent, CPA, and financial advisor, I suggest that you find new professionals to be on your Money Team. Why? You want to make sure the people on your team are loyal to you and have your best interests at heart. You might not feel comfortable being 100% transparent with someone who is still on your ex's Money Team!

QUESTIONS TO CONSIDER & ACTION ITEMS:

Who is currently on your Money Team?

Are you happy with their performance and level of advice?

Who is missing from your Money Team?

Are you sitting down with the members of your Money Team at least annually?

Based on your answers to these questions, fill the gaps on your Money Team.

Part Two

Money Thoughts, Words, and Emotions

Chapter 8

NAME YOUR MONEY PAIN

*M*oney itself is rarely the root cause of divorce. Rather, it's the arguments over how the money is handled and the way you communicate (or don't communicate) about financial matters.

Most money arguments are actually disagreements over **values**. If you value something, you'll spend money on it. For example, a woman who values her appearance might choose to spend money on designer clothes, makeup, fancy cars, and even plastic surgery. Someone who values education will spend money on books, classes, private school for her children, and advanced degrees or certifications. Women who highly value entertainment and adventure will spend money on exotic vacations, fancy dinners out, or throwing expensive parties. None of these values are necessarily right or wrong. But when you and your spouse or partner have values that are diametrically opposed, conflict is bound to arise and money is pulled into the middle of it.

What's the deep-rooted money pain that divorce has left with you? I felt taken advantage of and disrespected by Jeff, especially when it came to the finances. I worked hard and made decent money right out of college. It felt unfair that I did all the work while Jeff did whatever he wanted to do. Of course, I realize now that I allowed this situation to continue. I never enforced consequences when Jeff screwed up by getting fired or arrested for driving drunk. I begrudgingly took those financial consequences onto myself, and then seethed in a stew of resentment. This is classic codependent behavior, as I later learned from my counselor, Dave. I became a financial enabler, and it was all my own fault.

At the time, I didn't respect myself or my money. If I had, I would have allowed Jeff to reap the consequences of his own misbehaviors. He either would have learned the lesson that I was unavailable to be his personal banker and changed his ways, or he would have moved on to someone else who would financially enable him. (I learned several years ago that he's repeating this pattern with another woman, which is no surprise.)

What are some other examples of money pain you might be feeling? Several women I've coached express a sense of not being worthy, not just of love, but also of money. Women who have caught their partner cheating, gambling, or secretly spending money often experience a lack of trust and betrayal. Partners of workaholics report feeling marginalized and unimportant. If a woman remained home to care for children and the household, her husband might have said or implied that her contribution wasn't as valuable as his, because he made the money.

It's absolutely vital for you to remember: **Sometimes money is used as a weapon, but it is *not* our enemy!** It would be easy for me to say that Jeff and I called off our wedding because of money fights. But the real reason I left him was because of his emotional manipulation, lack of responsibility, and disrespect of me. It was never about the money, yet it was always at the center of our conflicts, like a third person in the relationship. I suspect the same may be true for you.

QUESTIONS TO CONSIDER:

What's the root cause for your money pain?

What did you tolerate that you shouldn't have in regards to money in your former relationship?

Chapter 9

HOW HAS YOUR VIEW OF MONEY CHANGED SINCE DIVORCE?

ecause of the level of financial chaos in my relationship, my view of money *improved* after I split with my ex-fiancé, Jeff. Once I put some distance between us and sought counseling, I saw how I allowed my ex to take advantage of both me and money. When I didn't have a grown man-child to take care of, there was enough money to cover my necessities, with leftovers.

Money (my new best friend) and I began to start building up our savings, paying down our debt, and buying fun things and experiences we couldn't previously afford. It was a freeing and exhilarating experience to be in a relationship with my money without anxiety, stress, or guilt.

If you were the breadwinner, you might feel resentful that your former partner wasn't pulling their weight and all the financial responsibility was on you. Like me, it's possible you feel relieved and hopeful about the future of your finances.

However, maybe you're experiencing the opposite. If your ex earned a high income, you might feel abandoned by money, like the rug has been pulled out from under you. It can be a hard adjustment to make if you can no longer afford the lifestyle to which you were once accustomed. You might feel ashamed or judged by family or friends. If your ex earned a great deal more than you, perhaps money was used to control you.

If your ex managed the finances, it's possible you feel awkward in money's presence, not sure how to interact with it. Women tell me they feel stupid admitting they don't know the basics of personal finance, and find it hard to reach out for help and guidance.

As Jen Sincero states in her book, *You Are a Badass at Making Money*, "Money provides freedom and options." Therefore, money is a source of power. As women, it's important that we embrace this fact and unlock our own financial power. You and money can do a great deal of generous and wonderful things together, so long as your relationship is not dysfunctional.

This is why it's important to examine your situation and recognize how your view of money has changed since your divorce or breakup.

QUESTIONS TO CONSIDER:

How has your perception of money changed since divorce?

Has your view and experience of money improved or worsened?

How did money affect the power balance in your former relationship?

What sort of freedom and options would you like money to provide for you going forward?

Chapter 10

WHY MONEY IS SO EMOTIONAL

*M*oney is emotional because we're human, and humans are emotional creatures. You experience emotions in every area of your life, so why would money be an exception? But when left unexamined, your emotions have the potential to create financial chaos.

Most money experts will tell you, "If you want to change your financial results, you need to change your actions." Then they will give you a checklist of *7 Simple Steps to Financial Freedom*. They're partially right. If you take better actions with your money, you'll get better results.

ACTION -> RESULTS

But there's a big piece missing in this equation: **Emotion** is the trigger for the action we take. People usually take action for one of two reasons: to increase pleasure (positive emotions) or to decrease pain (negative emotions). And although it seems like our emotions come out of nowhere, there's a trigger for them, too.

EMOTION -> ACTION -> RESULT

Emotions—both positive and negative ones—are a reaction to what is going on around us and inside of us. If you're angry, it's because either someone said something you don't like or you're thinking about a situation that's upsetting to you. There's an underlying reason, a trigger, for the emotions we feel. Words— either spoken aloud or thought in your head—precede your emotions.

WORDS -> EMOTION -> ACTION -> RESULT

If you think about the last time you got angry, what happened right before that? Were you rehearsing some situation that happened? Did you get into an argument with your ex? Did a coworker say something rude and you reacted in anger? If I asked you right now to think about the last time someone made you angry, you could probably feel it again in your body, right? There might be thoughts and emotions simmering right beneath the surface that can cause us to repel money, and we're not even aware of them.

Your thoughts form your words, and words give birth to your emotions. Your thoughts and words directly affect how you feel about your finances. Your feelings drive your decisions and the resulting actions of your money management. The good news is that it's possible to harness the power of your emotions to achieve your financial goals, rather than wrestling against them.

The one thing we don't want to do is try to repress our emotions. If we do, they can spring out like an evil jack-in-the-box. This is why I hate when I hear of a financial professional telling women to "leave emotion out of your money decisions." It's literally impossible to do, and science has proven this.

Neuroscientist Antonio Damasio made a groundbreaking discovery: Humans *cannot* make logical decisions. It's literally impossible. He studied individuals with stroke damage in the part of the brain where emotions are generated. They seemed normal, except they were not able to express or interpret emotions. But Damasio found they all had something else in common: They couldn't make decisions. These individuals described what they might do in logical terms. Yet they couldn't make even simple choices, like whether to have a chicken sandwich or a hamburger for lunch. Damasio discovered the moment of decision occurs in the same part of the brain that processes emotion.

It's vital to understand what's going on beneath the surface in your mind. Your brain is like an iceberg. The part you're aware of, the conscious mind, is the tip of the iceberg. The unconscious mind, which drives 95% of our daily decisions, is hiding under the waters of our awareness. When you're talking about your finances, the things above the surface, things you're aware of, are your income, net worth, credit card debt, investments, cash in the bank, and expenses. But down beneath the surface, there are things affecting our financial behaviors that we don't always see. These things are negative self-talk, emotional triggers, unconscious patterns, money narratives, relationship dynamics, and maybe even financial trauma. My goal is to help you lower the waterline on the iceberg, so you can uncover what's going on beneath the surface to see what's driving your behavior.

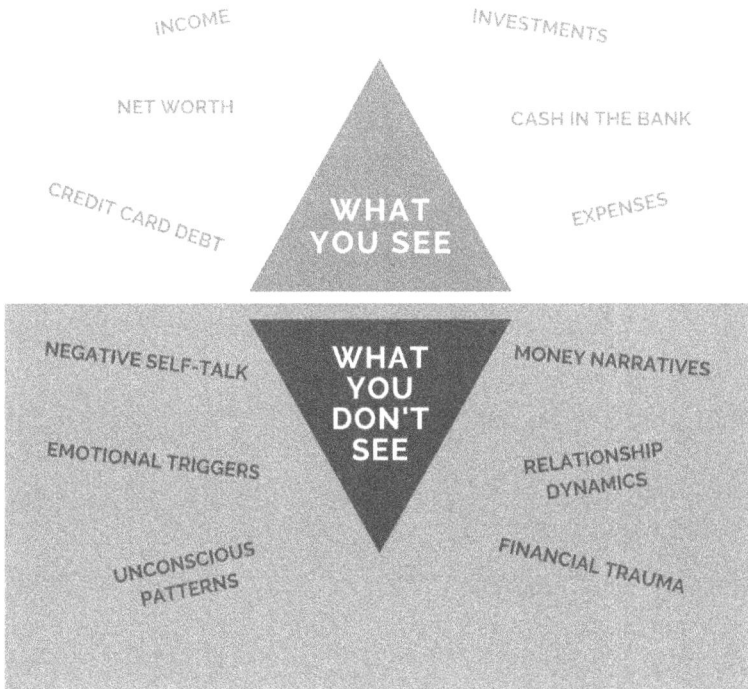

WHAT YOU SEE

INCOME   INVESTMENTS   NET WORTH   CASH IN THE BANK   CREDIT CARD DEBT   EXPENSES

WHAT YOU DON'T SEE

NEGATIVE SELF-TALK   MONEY NARRATIVES   EMOTIONAL TRIGGERS   RELATIONSHIP DYNAMICS   UNCONSCIOUS PATTERNS   FINANCIAL TRAUMA

When you were born, you had zero opinions about money, positive or negative. You began with a blank slate. As you moved through childhood and adulthood, you collected and processed information about money and stored it in your unconscious mind. You made it mean something based on your experiences.

Here's another way to think about money and your unconscious mind that I learned from author T. Harv Eker: like a blueprint. If I were to give you a blueprint for a ranch house, it doesn't matter how hard or fast you work, what building materials you buy, or who you hire. You're only going to get a ranch house using that blueprint; you're never going to get a two-story house. The only way you'll get a two-story house is if you go back and change the blueprint. I've found that many women are trying to build the equivalent of a two-story financial house, and yet they don't realize they're operating with a ranch blueprint. You don't need to work any harder or any faster. You need to go and correct the blueprint first. Once the blueprint is fixed, the outside actions and results come so much easier and faster than you would ever imagine.

Money becomes entangled with many types of emotional baggage as we move through life. It's time to start paying attention to the meaning we've given money, good or bad, so we can begin to untangle it.

ACTION ITEM:

Start paying attention to the thoughts you have and the words you speak about money.

Chapter 11

THE BOUNCER IN YOUR BRAIN

hat have you been thinking and saying about money? I want you to really listen to yourself. Have you been saying things like "I suck at managing my money," or "I'm not a numbers person," or "Making money is hard for me"? How do you feel about your finances right now, especially when you say those kinds of things? Why is our money self-talk so important? Why does it matter?

There's a part of your brain called the Reticular Activating System, or RAS, which acts as a filter in your brain. There are billions of bits of information coming at you every single second. If you didn't have the Reticular Activating System, your brain couldn't handle the number of stimuli coming at you. This is your brain's safety mechanism so you don't end up like a little puddle of Jell-O on the floor because of overwhelm.

I want you to think of the Reticular Activating System as your brain's bouncer. Whatever is important to you goes on the "guest list," and the RAS lets those things into your awareness. If something is not important to you, or if it's something you disagree with consciously or unconsciously, it will be denied entry. Because of this, your Reticular Activating System will filter out stimuli that contradict your deeply held convictions. So if you say things like "I'm no good with money" or "Making money is really hard," your RAS will literally block out opportunities contrary to those beliefs. There might be a potential situation for you to make money that's relatively easy and effortless. *Your brain will not even allow you to see it* because your unconscious mind wants you to agree with yourself at its very core.

Scientists have conducted studies with people to see how the RAS filters out information in the environment based on beliefs. They told one group of people, "You are very lucky. You are so lucky, you even find money just lying on the street." The other group, the control group, wasn't told anything about being lucky. A few days later, they had each of the individuals in both groups walk down a certain stretch of street where the researchers placed a $20 bill on the ground. Upwards of 80% of the people who were told they were lucky spotted and picked up the money. It was completely the opposite with the control group. Only about 20% of those people saw and found the money, *even though it was in the exact same spot for everyone!* That's because our Reticular Activating System lets in what we focus on. That's why it is so important to make sure your words about money line up with the results you want.

Now that you know you make emotional money decisions and your brain might be working against you, are you doomed to fail with your finances? Not at all! I'm going to show you how to work *with* your emotions, rather than fighting against them. You'll find out how to super-charge your money goals with positive emotions, so you'll *want* to do the right thing. You'll also discover techniques for quickly releasing your negative emotions, so they're not working against you financially.

But first you need to uncover what you're thinking and saying about your finances. When it comes to money, *think about what you've been thinking about.* What are you saying to yourself—both out loud and in your head—when it comes to money? Are you saying things like this?

- "That's too expensive."
- "I'll never pay off my student loans."
- "I'll never make enough money to support myself."
- "I don't understand investing."

Pay special attention to the words you are using when you find yourself getting emotional about money. Do you notice any trends in your negative money statements? What negative things did your ex say about money?

ACTION ITEM:

Write down at least ten negative things you think or say about money.

Chapter 12

MONEY STORIES

*A*t times, you're not sure why certain financial emotions, thoughts, and actions are plaguing you. They seem to be irrational and you don't know their source. All of us have money stories or narratives from our past, usually from our childhood years, which color our present financial behaviors.

These money narratives contain *some* grain of truth and might have served a useful purpose for you in the past. However, when your money stories contain some falsehood or aren't applicable to your current situation, they can harm your financial health. These half-truths about money are typically passed down to us from our parents or other family members.

According to Brad Klontz and Rick Kahler, the authors of *Facilitating Financial Health*: *Tools for Financial Planners, Coaches, and Therapists*, when people find themselves repeating the same painful mistakes around money, there's usually unresolved emotional pain stemming from a past event or relationship.

How do you unearth your money stories? The negative things you think and say about money are clues. Maybe you say or think things like "It's hard for me to make money. I'm not organized. I'm not good at math. Making money is hard," You probably heard it from someone else, either in your childhood or maybe even in your marriage. If an important person in your life tells you something repeatedly, you eventually believe it as your truth.

What is your earliest or most vivid money memory from your childhood? Did your father make you feel bad because he gave you a dollar for the ice cream truck, and you lost it? Maybe you were yelled at, and your dad told you, "Money doesn't grow on trees. I worked really hard for that money. How could you be so careless?"

Typically, your money stories come from the words, actions, and attitudes of the important adults in your life. As a child, you look to your parents and other authority figures in your life for information about how the world – and money – works. You're just absorbing all this information as a young child. When we're very young, we see our parents as the ultimate authority on everything. And many times, we take what they say as absolute truth. Most of us have multiple money stories. But one usually pops to the surface more readily when you start to examine your negative self-talk or think about your most vivid money memory.

Let's talk about the difference between a child's brain and an adult's brain, because this is vitally important. Children's brains are biologically different from adult brains while awake. Adults are usually in a state of either alpha or beta brainwaves. Alpha brain waves are a restful, creative state, and beta brain waves are an active problem-solving mode. However, children between the ages of two and seven are different.

They are primarily in a state of theta brainwaves while they're awake. Theta brainwaves are a "super learning state" when the brain acts like a sponge, absorbing and storing massive amounts of information directly into the unconscious mind. Children in theta brain wave states are typically very open to suggestion and are likely to accept what you tell them as the truth. If you have a child and remember the four-to-five-year-old range, you might have even said, "My kid is like a sponge! She just absorbs everything."

At this age, if you accidentally slip up and say a curse word, they'll repeat it three days later in public in the proper context (to your horror). The reason is biological. Young children have to learn massive amounts of information in order to survive in this world. They have to learn how to interact and fit into the family unit, and into the different parts of society. You might have heard that young children can learn to speak multiple languages at the same time, with the same ease of learning just one. You could teach a child English, German, and Spanish at age four, and, thanks to the theta brainwave state, they'll learn it easier than an adult who's 24.

All of this information about how to get along in the world, how to interact socially, and learning language is all absorbed down into the unconscious mind and stored there. Plus, children at this age don't have the judgment to reject something and say, "I don't think that's true. I'm not going to believe that," the way adults do. This is why you can tell your child that there's a secret fairyland out in the garden outside your house, and they will believe you. Can you see the potential problem here?

If your parents or other authority figures told you false or negative things about money, you, as a child, stored it in your unconscious mind as the truth, never to be examined again. It's part of your "money blueprint," so to speak. It's the way you operate without even thinking. When are adults in a state of theta brainwaves? In the "twilight" period between wakefulness and sleep, or when you're under hypnosis! It's important to keep this in mind if you want to reprogram your negative thoughts and overwrite them with a positive narrative. Doing mindset work first thing in the morning or right before you go to bed are the most effective times to do it, because you're closer to the theta brainwave state.

One of my divorcing clients, Carrie, felt nervous about her lack of retirement savings. She told me she couldn't control her spending. Carrie said, "Whenever I get any money, I feel like it's my money and I should get to spend it on whatever I want to. But at the same time, I understand my lack of retirement savings is also causing me stress. I just don't know how to make myself set aside money for my retirement. It's like I have this compulsion to spend it!"

I asked her to write down the negative things she was thinking and saying about money. I asked her to reflect on her early money memories. When Carrie came back to our next coaching session, she said, "Ah-ha! I figured out where that story came from. I remember my mother taking my brothers and me school shopping for my first day of kindergarten. Mom drove us to one of the discount department stores, usually Sears or JC Penney. She had a very strict budget for each of us children. We needed to buy a certain number of shirts and pants, and we couldn't go over the set dollar amount. I asked for a dress I wanted, which was outside of the budget. Mom told me, 'There's not enough money, so you can't have it.' After we finished with our school shopping, she took us to the other side of the mall, to the high-end department stores to shop for herself. I asked her, 'Mom, I didn't think we had any money left. How come we can only spend a set amount, but you get to buy whatever you want to?' My mom said, 'Carrie, when you're an adult and you make your own money, then you can spend it on whatever you want to.'"

Carrie continued, "As soon as I landed my first job as a teenager and started making my own money, that's what I lived by. My mantra has been: *I'm an adult, I'm making my own money. I can spend my money on whatever I want.* And I did. I spent it all. I was not a good saver or an investor." And I said, "Well, you know what? You are an adult. And of course, you can spend your money however you want to, but you can also make the choice to save whatever you want to as well."

We came up with some practical strategies to put Carrie's saving and investing on autopilot. But we also made sure she didn't feel deprived, having a set amount of fun money every month to spend on whatever she wanted to. But just the realization of where the pattern came from, helped to remove the block keeping her from saving money.

Now that you know why your unproductive money stories exist, it's time to identify and revisit these sometimes painful memories. This step must be completed before you can fully embrace a new way of handling money. When you uncover these narratives and examine them objectively, you can make a proactive decision as to whether they are helping or hindering your journey to financial health. You can then rewrite your money stories to have happy endings.

Here are some common money stories women tell themselves:

- If I had more money, life would be so much better.
- Money is evil (or dirty or bad).
- I don't deserve more money.
- I deserve to spend all the money I want.
- You have to work really hard for money.
- There will never be enough money.
- Money isn't important to me.
- Financial success will make me important.
- Good girls don't pursue money (or talk about it).
- If I'm a good person, God/the Universe will take care of me.

Left unexamined, these money narratives and emotionally charged events of your past can continue to haunt you and harm you, forming impassable roadblocks on your journey to Financial Dignity®. For some, counseling or therapy is beneficial and necessary to heal these emotional wounds. In fact, one of the first things I did when I broke off my engagement with Jeff was to seek counseling. I knew I was operating out of a dysfunctional mindset, and I needed the help of a counselor to rewrite them with happy endings.

QUESTIONS TO CONSIDER & ACTION ITEMS:

Write down one or more memories from your childhood that may still be affecting the way you view money and wealth.

Do you see yourself, or your parents, in any of these money stories?

If so, does a particular money memory that is especially strong come to mind for you? Write it down and consider it objectively.

Did this money story fit the past situation?

Is it helping or hurting your current financial situation?

Chapter 13

WRITING A LETTER TO MONEY

Money is the third person in your marriage. It became tangled in the drama of your relationship. But it's not money's fault! You might have residual negativity, shame, or trauma attached to money that you need to release. Because unlike your ex, you and money are still together, forever! You can't have true Financial Dignity® without a positive relationship with your money.

The first step to healing is to express your fears and feelings in order to clear out the negativity. I want you to write a letter to money and say all of the things that are on your heart and mind.

If I had written a letter to money when I broke up with Jeff, it would have sounded like this:

Dear Money,

I am SO sorry for all the ways I let you down and mistreated you over the past seven years. I allowed Jeff to talk me into spending you on his alcohol and weed. I let him borrow you to bail him out of both his money messes and his legal messes, rather than keep you safe in the bank. I know you wanted to protect me and take care of me. But I dragged you into seedy situations like bounced checks, pawn shops, and payday loans. I didn't stand up for us, but allowed Jeff to mistreat us both. I'm sorry I didn't leave sooner.

And most of the time, I blamed you. There wasn't enough of you to go around to pay the bills. If I just had more of you, then life would be okay. The truth is, more of you would have only magnified and prolonged the problem. I have lots of regrets about how I have treated you in the past, Money. I promise, I am going to do everything I can to make it up to you. So please stay with me and let me try again.

~ Christine

Writing your letter to money uncovers your fears and regrets around your personal finances. Many women tell me they feel lighter just getting those feelings off their chest. It's also a valuable exercise for uncovering those faulty money stories lurking beneath the surface. I'm going to give you the exact formula to create your new Magnetic Money Mantras™ to help you overwrite the negative patterns you'll discover as a result of your letter to money. And hang onto this letter, because you're going to need it for a future exercise in this book.

ACTION ITEM:

Write your letter to money as if it's a person. (Do NOT skip this exercise!)

Part Three

DANGEROUS EMOTIONAL MONEY BEHAVIORS

Chapter 14

Using Money as a Weapon

*A*nger is one of the stages of grief and you will probably experience it multiple times during the divorce process. The trick is to allow the anger to move through you in a productive way, without hurting yourself or others. Unfortunately, I see women using money as a weapon. In this scenario, you use money to inflict harm on your former spouse or partner out of anger. It's the fight response to stress. If you're tempted to do this, remember anger is a two-edged sword that cuts both ways.

Several years ago, I chatted with a frustrated financial planner who unsuccessfully attempted to talk his client "down from the ledge" regarding her money decisions. As part of her divorce settlement, this woman received half of her husband's 401(k) funds. She reasoned that because the "no-good-bastard" cheated on her with her best friend, she deserved to spend $50,000 of "his retirement money" on a red BMW convertible. Every time she drove her "revenge car" to his house to pick up or drop off their kids, it would be a rub in his face.

Her financial planner pleaded with her not to withdraw $50,000 from the 401(k) to buy the convertible, but his client, in her anger, wouldn't listen. By cashing out part of the 401(k) money, she owed taxes and penalties, to the tune of 40%, a $20,000 tax bill! This means the convertible essentially cost her $70,000!

The withdrawal also meant she had substantially less money for her retirement. A quick run through an investment calculator would show her the $50,000 invested at 8% over 20 years would be worth $233,000 at retirement. Yikes! How do you like that car now?

Of course, this woman's anger is justified. But what would be a better course of action if you're feeling this way right now? Talk to a counselor or therapist as a constructive outlet for your anger. Take up a physically taxing form of exercise like kickboxing, running, weight training, or CrossFit. This provides the angry energy in your body a positive outlet that actually benefits you. And go ahead and spend a reasonable amount of money on yourself as a reward for making it through the divorce! Rather than buying a $50,000 Mercedes, maybe my friend's client could've spent $5,000 on a Louis Vuitton handbag or a yoga retreat in Bali. She would've had a sense of satisfaction without the major financial damage!

"I wish people had a longer-term perspective of what the divorce really means," says James Lenhoff, CFP®, and Co-founder of Wealthquest. "I think women see the divorce as the end of the relationship. It's actually the beginning of a new, and very strange version of the relationship. Your ex will still be very much a part of your life, especially if you have kids. You need to be prepared for how you'll think and feel in that new version of the relationship. Money can become a weapon, and it can be used as a weapon for a very long time in this new stage." James adds,

"You need to know how that works and be ready for it, if your ex decides to use it against you."

When you see red and lash out financially at the height of your anger, you're putting yourself in dangerous territory. Give yourself 24 hours to calm down before you respond. No one wins when money is used as a weapon, even if you're the one wielding it. Revenge clouds your judgment, poisons your emotions, and taints your relationship with money. Your long-term success with money is truly the best "revenge."

QUESTIONS TO CONSIDER & ACTION ITEMS:

Are you feeling angry at your ex?

In what ways are you tempted to hurt your ex with money?

How might this backfire on you in the long run?

What activity can you do to physically release your anger in a productive way?

Put it on the calendar, and go do it!

Chapter 15

GIVING AWAY THE STORE

When I left Jeff, I "gave away the store." I was done arguing and fighting. I just wanted to get away from him, our shared apartment, and everything in it, as fast as possible. In doing so, I cost myself money. Because, if Jeff said he wanted something, I just let him have it. In fact, I only took a few things from the apartment besides my clothes, books, and jewelry. I left him almost all of our furniture and our pets (which completely broke my heart, especially leaving my dog Bronx behind). This is known as the flight response to stress.

Since Jeff and I were only engaged, the court didn't divide up our assets or our debt. Because Jeff had terrible credit, all of the debt remained in my name. Did I even try to get him to take responsibility for any of it? No. Jeff's vehicle was titled in my name due to his two DUI offenses. My counselor encouraged me to sell it to help pay off my debt. "I can't do that!" I protested. "That's Jeff's car!"

My counselor asked me: "Whose name is on the title? Whose insurance is covering the car?" Mine. Unfortunately, I didn't take my counselor's advice. It seemed mean, and I wasn't mean, even in the midst of a major breakup. So I gave Jeff an ultimatum. Get the car out of my name in 30 days, or I'm coming to get it. Of course, he still acted like I was being unreasonable. I realize now how weak and flimsy my personal boundaries were back then. Even now, I think of things I wish I hadn't left behind. Maybe you're tired of fighting, too. Trust me, I understand. It can feel exhausting! But there are things worth taking a stand for during your divorce.

I find that many women struggle with healthy confrontation and avoid it entirely. As a society, women have been conditioned to cooperate, to get along, to be agreeable. Otherwise, we're labeled as bitches or ball-busters for enforcing our boundaries.

"I wish I'd seen more role models in my culture handle money in an empowered way," says Cindy Alisha Gunraj, a divorce coach. "Most of the time, men controlled the finances, and women were left out of the money discussions. Men used it as a form of dominance and control. I remember my own mother telling me 'Don't take too much,' in my own divorce settlement!"

Fortunately, this is beginning to change, and we can teach our daughters, nieces, and granddaughters how to respectfully maintain healthy boundaries in relationships. Here's the lesson: *It's important to stand up for yourself especially if you shy away from confrontation.*

You need to be assertive to receive your fair share of both the money and personal belongings. Child support and custody agreements can be difficult and challenging to revise later, so it's important to stick to your guns and get what you deserve the first time around. A good divorce attorney will help you with this, especially if you're the type of woman who, like me, dislikes conflict and drama.

Marriage and family therapist Emma Viglucci says, "I find that women who are going for a divorce tend to feel disempowered when it comes to finances. They end up putting up with inappropriate treatment and settling just to be done with the process. It's vital for divorcing women to fully own and honor themselves and be vigilant with their boundaries."

If you're finding it hard to advocate for yourself, try this technique. Advocate for a higher cause. Even the kindest, gentlest woman turns into a grizzly momma bear if you mess with her kids. Every dollar you don't get is money you don't get to spend taking care of your kids. What if you don't have kids? Identify your higher cause, which might be the homeless shelter or the ASPCA. If you're struggling financially because you haven't stood up for yourself during divorce, that's less money you have to donate to your favorite charity.

Even if you're tempted to flee the relationship, "Don't rush things," cautions Kim West, a divorce coach. "Take the time up front to prepare, learn what all of your options are, and find out what resources you can leverage to get through the process in a way that aligns with your goals. There are so many potential mistakes, so I recommend hiring divorce industry professionals such as a CDFA® and a divorce coach to assist you."

QUESTIONS TO CONSIDER:

Are you someone who goes along with what other people want to avoid conflict?

Is there a financial issue that you need to take a stand on?

What's at stake if you don't advocate for yourself?

Enlist the help of your attorney, if you need to!

Chapter 16

DEER IN THE HEADLIGHTS

ou're driving down a country road on a summer night, radio blaring, singing at the top of your lungs. You round a curve, and your headlights land on a deer – standing in the middle of the road, staring straight at you. Your adrenaline spikes as you slam on your brakes and the horn simultaneously, yelling, "Augghh! Move!" After a long second, the deer finally bolts out of the way, narrowly missing your car.

Are you reacting to the process of divorce like a deer in the headlights? Frozen in fear, afraid to move? This happens when you feel paralyzed and unable to take productive action. This is known as the freeze response to stress and can actually be worse than fight (using money as a weapon) or flight (giving away the store).

Most women who experience the freeze response did not initiate the divorce. If this is you, you might be in a state of shock or denial. But refusing to make decisions *is a decision.* Delaying action can force you into an unfavorable course of action by default. Interestingly, the "deer in the headlights" response has two potential causes: overwhelm and confusion. The problem is that both of them can manifest as fear. "And," says Holistic Divorce Coach, Olga Nadal, "combining fear and money makes your divorce process longer and more painful!"

How can you tell which one it is? If more information will help you move forward in the divorce process, then you're probably confused about the right action to take. If more information feels like it would make the problem worse, you're experiencing overwhelm.

If confusion is the cause of your inaction, determine exactly what you need to know and find the right source of information or expert to help you. Don't be ashamed or embarrassed to reach out to your attorney or financial planner to ask questions. That's their job, and they work for you!

If you are overwhelmed, talk to your attorney or financial professional, and ask them to give you baby steps. Explain that you're overwhelmed and a mile-long To-Do list from them stresses you out and causes you to procrastinate. If the financial piece is causing you overwhelm, consider hiring a financial coach or even a daily money manager to hold your hand through this transition. If your overwhelm is growing into larger issues like anxiety or panic attacks, please seek the help of a mental health professional. But whatever you do, do not remain frozen in the middle of the road! We all know what happens to the poor dear who does.

QUESTIONS TO CONSIDER & ACTION ITEMS:

Do you currently feel like a deer in the headlights, unable to take productive action to move your divorce forward?

Will more information help you, or will it make you feel overwhelmed?

Talk to your attorney and financial pros, and ask them to give you baby steps if you're overwhelmed. If you're confused, ask them for clarification and more information. Remember, they work for you!

Chapter 17

SECRET KEEPING

our secrets make you sick. If you have a history of hiding money, debt, or assets from your ex, it's either because of shame or a lack of trust. In fact, this could be one of the reasons for your divorce. Unfortunately, I hear horror stories about ex-spouses with secret credit cards or gambling debt on a regular basis.

If you are the one hiding spending, debt, shopping, or gambling, it's because this behavior has become out of control and you're feeling shameful as a result. These reckless behaviors are not driven by money, but rather by dysfunctional emotions or even addictions. Money is the arena in which these root issues are appearing. Your money is the location, so to speak, but not the cause. Therapy is usually necessary to uncover the root and constructively deal with these out-of-control behaviors.

If you are hiding cash, savings accounts, or other assets or investments, the reason is typically a lack of trust. I know because I lived this way for seven years. I always hid money from Jeff because I didn't trust him to leave it in the bank for our bills. I felt guilty for lying to him, but my need for self-preservation trumped those feelings. Most women, me included, have a high need for safety and security. Adequate savings in the bank makes me relax, knowing financial emergencies can be handled when they happen. I hated living paycheck to paycheck, in constant fear of not having enough money to pay the bills. So, I secretly squirreled money away on the rare occasion I could.

When an emergency happened, and I pulled out my secret stash to take care of it, Jeff would lash out at me for hiding money from him. I would remind him if I hadn't, we'd be up a crap creek without a paddle. Of course, yelling and drama invariably ensued. It got to the point where Jeff would badger me for money, asking if I was hiding any from him. Honestly, the whole thing was freaking exhausting. Maybe you can relate?

If secret-keeping was modeled by your parents while you were growing up, you might think it's normal. Maybe you witnessed your parents fighting because one of them hid spending or savings from the other. Maybe your mom would take you shopping but tell you not to let your dad know how much she spent on you. Maybe your father would secretly slip you cash and whisper, "Let's keep this between us." It's easy to repeat the patterns of the past without questioning whether or not those behaviors are serving us well today.

Just as there are little white lies and big fat lies, there's also a spectrum of secret-keeping. You've never had a secret credit card or gambling debt, but you might have a few small money secrets you're keeping. You might "forget" to tell your partner about something you charged on the credit card or a small bonus you received at work because you want to spend it on yourself alone.

Communicating openly and honestly with your partner – especially about money - is the key to a good relationship. And chances are, at some point in the future, you will be in another one. That's why it's important to determine if secret-keeping is an unhealthy financial pattern for you.

When you're not honest about the state of your personal finances, you're also lying to yourself, which is dangerous. Why? Because dishonesty breeds dysfunction. We tell ourselves lies about our money all the time. "I don't have a college degree, so I'll never make a decent income." "I'm not a numbers person; I'll never be good with money." "I'm a single mom, so I'm always going to struggle." "I'm a free spirit, so I'll never be able to stick to a budget."

Here's the truth: Every day, we are choosing, consciously or unconsciously, how we use (or misuse) money. We need to take a good, hard look at how we are earning, spending, and saving (or not saving) our money. When we tell ourselves lies about the state of our finances, we feel better momentarily. But things will NOT change for the better until we change our behavior around money.

No one else can change your relationship with money for the better except for you. It starts with taking ownership.

QUESTIONS TO CONSIDER:

Was there any secret-keeping surrounding money in your previous relationship? If so, please explain.

What about in your parents' relationship?

What lies do you tell yourself about money?

Do you know how much you are spending and saving each month?

Will you commit to being honest with yourself about the state of your finances from now on?

Chapter 18

VICTIM THINKING

"You can be pitiful or you can be powerful, but you can't be both," says my spiritual mentor, Joyce Meyer.

Yes, your ex might be to blame (at least in part) for the current state of your finances, but remaining in victim mode isn't productive. You can't move forward and make positive money changes if you remain in victim mode. You have a choice. You can waste energy blaming others, or you can use that energy constructively, making a plan to improve your money situation.

It's easier in the short term to blame the current state of your money on your ex. The inner and outer changes needed to become financially healthy take effort. When I first broke up with Jeff, I played the victim. He helped me charge up my credit cards, and he didn't pay me back. Jeff always came up short for his share of the monthly bills, which is why I depleted my savings account. Jeff never paid me back the money I lent him for bail when he racked up two DUIs in six months.

I could continue for days with the "he always" and "he never" stories. Certainly, my friends and family felt pity for me and my situation. But pity and sympathy don't pay the bills! I realized it was time for me to shed the cocoon of blame and emerge as the money victor, instead of being a money victim.

This step is key to owning your financial power and healing your relationship with money. No, you can't control everything that happens to you. But you can control your response to it. You can choose to be upset, to blame, to rage, and to feel pitiful. None of those things will improve your financial situation.

The most powerful thing you can do is to claim "From now on, I take ownership of my finances. I am in charge of my money, and I choose to manage it wisely."

QUESTIONS TO CONSIDER:

What money woes are you blaming on your ex?

Are you a money victim? Are you ready to shed this identity and become a money victor?

What scares you about giving up your tendency to blame others for your money messes?

Chapter 19

EMOTIONAL SPENDING

*E*veryone indulges in emotional spending from time to time. I mentioned that decisions are made in the same region of the brain that processes emotion. So literally, all of your buying decisions are emotional at some level. The problem occurs when you're spending money from a place of overwhelm and negativity, rather than a place of peacefulness and positivity.

Emotional spending occurs when you buy something to make yourself feel better, not because you need the item. It's easy to justify the purchase, "I've had a rough day/week/month, so I deserve to treat myself."

We've all known women who get divorced and return to partying and bar-hopping like they did in their college days for a period of time. Other women turn to shopping for comfort or as a distraction, rather than face the emotional pain of divorce. "Retail therapy" is just a more socially acceptable form of self-soothing than downing an entire bottle of chardonnay on a weeknight.

Here's the problem: *The emotional pain you're trying to avoid will still be there after the shopping high has worn off and the credit card bills start rolling in.* In the same way that your wine-chugging friend wakes up to a physical hangover, your indulgence in retail therapy leaves you waking up to a financial hangover.

Here's the two-pronged strategy proven to help: counseling and mindful spending. Seek out a divorce support group or a counselor to help you constructively work through the painful issues of your divorce. Even if you initiated your divorce or breakup, you will go through the various stages of grief at the loss of the relationship. A divorce therapist will give you constructive ways to process your painful emotions so you won't need retail therapy.

Mindful spending is simply paying attention to your thoughts, words, and feelings when you're shopping. Before you even head to the store, decide what it is you need or want to buy and how much you intend to spend. One way to ensure you don't overspend is to leave your credit and debit cards at home and only take cash.

Pause and take a deep breath before you head to the register. Ask yourself these questions: Do I need this? Do I really want this? Will this truly bring me enjoyment — and for how long? Do I have the cash to pay for it? How am I feeling right now?

If you are shopping online, let your items sit in your virtual shopping cart and walk away from your computer. If possible, make yourself wait 24 hours before purchasing.

If you succumb to an episode of emotional spending, don't berate yourself for it. Instead, get curious. What happened right before the emotional spending occurred? What emotions were you experiencing? Were you rehearsing a drama-filled situation in your head?

I heard a story of a woman who treated herself to a new pair of shoes after every stressful encounter with her ex-husband. Since she shared custody of her kids with her ex, it happened often enough to cause an astronomical credit card balance and a shortage of closet space!

In order to stop emotional spending in its tracks, you need to identify three things: the trigger, the emotional need, and healthy alternatives.

Can you identify the triggers for your emotional spending? Which situations and who in particular "pushes your buttons"? It might not necessarily be your ex-spouse. I had a client with an overbearing and judgmental mother who tried being "helpful" during her daughter's divorce. The truth is that her mother's meddling stressed my client out more than dealing with her ex!

Sometimes it's not a negative emotion that triggers emotional spending, but rather a positive one. Maybe it's a fun shopping buddy or your favorite store or website that causes you to spend more than you intended.

Either way, emotional spending satisfies a legitimate emotional need in an unhealthy way. What are the good feelings you experience while shopping? Happiness, control, excitement, distraction? What feelings are you attempting to soothe with spending? Loneliness, frustration, anger, helplessness? Once you identify the feelings you want – and the ones you want to leave behind – you can devise healthy alternatives.

There are plenty of healthy alternatives to emotional spending, most of them costing little to no money. If you head to the stores to shop and interact with the salespeople because you're feeling lonely, invite a friend over for coffee or a glass of wine instead. Volunteer to cuddle kittens or puppies at your local animal shelter. If you shop as a response to stress, take a warm bath with lavender essential oil while listening to classical music. Meditate, do yoga, or go for a long walk in nature.

For my clients who struggle with emotional spending, I ask them to create a list of ten low-cost or no-cost ways to satisfy their emotional needs without shopping. I encourage you to do the same, and put it where you'll see it. The next time you feel sad, anxious, or angry, you'll have a list of activities to pick from to make yourself feel better quickly without running up your credit card balance.

QUESTIONS TO CONSIDER:

Are you an emotional spender?

Are you spending to numb negative emotions? What are you trying to avoid feeling?

What are your triggers and areas of temptation (types of purchases, stores, websites, shopping buddies)?

Chapter 20

CONTROL FREAK

H aving a healthy awareness of what's going on in your personal finances is my ultimate goal for you. You can get out of balance in two ways: by ignoring your money (the ostrich syndrome) or by obsessing over it (becoming a control freak). It's one thing to be in control of your money; it's quite another when you obsess over and micromanage the details.

When going through a divorce or major breakup, life can feel chaotic and out of control. You might take back control by being hyper-vigilant about where each and every penny goes. Yes, you should spend time managing your personal finances at least weekly, but it should not be an all-consuming part of your life.

If you're logging into your bank accounts multiple times per day, checking your credit more than once a month, or counting and recounting your cash constantly, you've crossed the line from being in control of your money to obsessively controlling it. If you have kids, you might also be freaking out over the money you spend on them, even reminding them on a regular basis that

"Mommy doesn't have money for that" or "Money doesn't grow on trees!"

Certainly, you have some changes happening in your financial situation because of the divorce, but if you are spending a large chunk of each day managing and worrying about your money, then you're out of balance.

When I dated Jeff, I was a money controller. I was always thinking about money, transferring money, paying bills, checking my account balances, and generally trying to keep Jeff from messing up my plan. (Which he did on a regular basis.)

If this is an issue for you, ask yourself what you're hoping to accomplish by expending all this effort into micromanaging your money. Some personality types are more prone to this type of controlling and obsessive worrying than others. If you feel unable to rein in the behavior on your own, enlist the help of a mental health professional.

What's a healthy balance look like when it comes to managing and checking on your personal finances? I spend about 20-30 minutes once a week checking my accounts, paying bills, and keeping tabs on my spending. Occasionally, I might check account balances in between my weekly "money dates," but only if I need to make a big purchase decision.

QUESTIONS TO CONSIDER:

Are you a control freak when it comes to your money? Do you check your accounts daily, or even several times a day?

How much time per day or per week do you spend on managing your personal finances?

Part Four

Repairing Your Relationship with Money

Chapter 21

Money Isn't the Enemy

*I*t's not uncommon for money to become entangled with trauma, especially if you are exiting a dysfunctional, abusive, or controlling relationship. It's estimated that financial abuse and control is present in upwards of 98% of abusive relationships. If money was used to punish, shame, or control you, it's vitally important to untangle the money from the trauma and abuse. Your ex is the real villain, not money. Money was just the pawn in the power game.

I recently chatted with another financial coach whose divorcing client said, "Money makes me sick; it's a prison, and I hate everything about it." This woman's husband emotionally abused her and used money to control her during their marriage. It's understandable that you might feel this way about money if it's been used as a weapon against you.

It reminds me of a scene from a movie or show I watched years ago (and I can't remember the source.) A mob boss captured and imprisoned an innocent woman in a cell and placed a formidable guard outside her door. The woman hated and feared both the mob boss and his guard. One day, the woman awoke to arguing outside of her cell. She peeked out the tiny window and witnessed the guard advocating for more food and another blanket for her. The mob boss accused the guard of getting soft and commanded his other goons to give him a beat-down to remind him of his place. Later, when the mob boss's fortress came under attack, the guard freed the woman and helped her escape.

If money was used to control you, your ex is the mob boss; money is the guard who's under the boss's control. Money is simply a tool in the hand of the person wielding it. Whether it's a helpful tool or a destructive weapon depends on whose hand it's in. Money itself is neutral, but it can get caught in the crossfire. You can easily associate the negative traits of your ex with money itself.

Money is like the third person in your relationship. You might view money as your captor that keeps you in your abusive relationship...or the savior who can free you from the tyrant. Money is not the enemy! It wants to have an amazing relationship with you. Money wants to take care of you and help support your happiness. But first, you have to believe it's true.

Kimmy*, a divorced woman who wishes to remain anonymous told me, "I was verbally abused for six long years. When you are told terrible things over and over, you start to believe them. It was such a dark time in my life. From a money perspective, I wanted out of my marriage so badly that I gave him way more money, home, and car than I should have."

There are times when it feels like money has betrayed or abandoned us, especially if your spouse had an affair and spent money on the other woman. Kim West, a divorce coach, says, "I discovered my husband was having an affair with and spending lots of money on another woman (a stripper, no less!) as well as grappling with serious substance abuse issues he'd been hiding from me. Not only had I lost trust in him, as well as others, but also in myself."

The exercises in this book will go a long way to untangling money from past trauma and negative beliefs. For some of us, this will require professional help, and that's nothing to be ashamed of. Repairing your relationship with money is a process that takes time and effort. Tools that can help this process include counseling and therapy, hypnosis, bodywork like Emotional Freedom Technique (a.k.a tapping) a Neuro Emotional Technique (NET), meditation, prayer, coaching, and self-reflection.

Like any relationship, your relationship with money will require ongoing maintenance. Unlike your ex, you and money will be together forever! Remember, money isn't the enemy. It wants to have an amazing relationship with you! Money wants to support your happiness, if you'll let it.

QUESTIONS TO CONSIDER:

Did your ex use money to hurt you or control you?

In what ways?

Can you see and accept that money isn't responsible for your pain?

Chapter 22

MANAGING EMOTIONS AROUND MONEY

"While going through divorce, I wish I had known how my emotions could be used against me to control my money habits. And I wish I had known that by taking charge of my emotions around money, I could empower myself when it came to my financial decisions," says Allison Dagney, author of the memoir *When Tears Leave Scars*.

Is there a trick to ensuring your emotions never get the best of you? It would certainly come in handy during divorce when emotionally upsetting things seem to happen every other day. Managing emotions with money is easier said than done, and it takes both intention and practice. Now that you know money is emotional, here's the million-dollar question: What do you do about it?

First, stop fighting with your emotions. Resisting and suppressing emotions around money causes them to spring forth in the form of tears, a panic attack, or an angry outburst at the worst possible time. When you don't allow your emotions to be expressed, they get stuck and don't go away. The best thing to do when you feel emotions rise up is to actually FEEL them in your body and allow them to pass.

Your feelings aren't bad or wrong. You have them for a reason. Your feelings are trying to tell you something. And you can learn from them if you listen, rather than ignore them. As Nancy Levin says in her book *Worthy: Boost Your Self-Worth to Grow Your Net Worth*, "You have feelings. You are not your feelings. They're visitors that stay for a short time and pass through."

Second, get curious about your emotions. If you're in the process of buying a new car and you feel fear, ask yourself why. Are you afraid the salesperson is judging you or taking advantage of you because you're not financially savvy? Are you afraid that if your income dropped, you won't be able to make the payment?

Examine the emotion and try to find the root of it. You'll usually discover one of two things: You're reliving a past emotion you didn't process (example: you were taken advantage of or shamed in another situation concerning a large purchase), or there is a legit financial concern you're trying to sweep under the rug.

If you continually experience the same emotions regarding your finances, it might be due to a faulty money story from your past. *It's worth the time and effort it takes to uncover and permanently rewrite these negative patterns.* Be sure you revisit Chapter 12, "Money Stories," and do the exercises, if you haven't already.

Finally, let emotions subside, and then decide. Financial mistakes can happen when you act in the heat of emotion, whether it's positive or negative. You might buy something based on excitement, only to regret the purchase later when the credit card bill comes in. When emotional "volume" is high, there's no room to hear wisdom from your logic. That's why it's best to *let emotions subside, and then decide.*

Give your emotions room to be expressed. Take the time you need to feel scared, sad, guilty, or even excited. Feel the emotions in your body, and give them space and time to pass. I always tell my clients to wait at least 24 hours before making a large purchase. It's amazing the clarity you have when you sleep on a financial decision. I recently followed my own advice when purchasing my new car. I had the money to purchase it on the spot, and I felt really good about the decision. But I still slept on it to ensure I was 100% positive. I went back the next day and bought it, no regrets!

I learned an intriguing notion called "emotional invincibility" from Hal Elrod, in his book *The Miracle Equation*. This technique can be applied to any emotionally upsetting situation, whether it's a money issue, divorce issue, work issue, or kid issue. I'll tell you exactly how it works, but know this: It takes practice. The more you practice on the little things, the easier it will be to apply it to the bigger and more upsetting issues.

When I first discovered this concept of emotional invincibility several years ago, I desperately needed to apply it to my business. When a potential ideal client decided not to hire me as their financial coach, I would go into a downward emotional spiral that lasted several days.

My head would spin with thoughts like "We're a perfect fit to work together! Why didn't they hire me? Am I charging too much? Maybe I should reach out and offer a discount? Maybe it was something I said? Or didn't say? God, I am such a horrible salesperson! If this customer didn't sign up, who's going to replace the lost revenue I was counting on? What if I never get another coaching client?"

When I remained stuck in those thoughts, my energy radiated negativity and doubt. Any emails or social media posts I created in that energy fell flat. This further proved the point that I sucked the big one and no one wanted to hire me. *But is it really the truth?* No.

It usually isn't my fault when someone decides not to work with me. The potential client who said no might be scared to hire a coach and invest the money. She might have a million things going on, so the timing isn't right. She might actually end up being a high-maintenance client, and her saying no is a blessing in disguise. The truth is I'm a damn good financial coach, and there are a hundred reasons why a person might choose to not work with me. And most of them don't have anything to do with me!

The emotional invincibility technique helps to bypass the downward spiral entirely by releasing the pressure valve on your emotions quickly.

Here's how it works:

- When something upsetting happens, set the timer on your phone for five minutes.
- You can rant, rave, scream, curse, or cry during the 5 minutes. Have your fit. It helps to physically release the emotional energy, rather than stuff it down inside where it festers.
- Once the timer goes off, stop what you're doing and say out loud, "I can't change it!" You can't change the upsetting thing that happened, so don't waste energy in your head trying to undo it.
- Now, put your effort and energy into something you *can* improve about the situation. If there's nothing constructive you can do right now, go relax and enjoy yourself.

When you first start practicing the steps above, you might need more than five minutes to throw your fit. If you typically spend days or weeks in an emotional fit, it might take 20 minutes for you to get it all out. What does applying emotional invincibility in a divorce situation look like? Here's a hypothetical, but all-too-common, scenario.

Your soon-to-be ex rejects your attorney's offer of a settlement amount that you feel is more than fair for both of you. You feel it coming: the upset, the rage, and all toxic thoughts pouring in about what a cheating, greedy S.O.B. he is. Grab your phone and set the timer for 5 minutes. Scream all the obscenities directed at your ex in your empty living room. Punch some pillows, scream, and cry. The phone alarm goes off.

Take a deep breath. And another. Say out loud, "I can't change it." Because it's true. You can't change the fact your husband and his attorney rejected the settlement offer. Now, is there something productive and helpful you can do? Once you're calm, call your attorney. Find out exactly what she recommends. Did he present a counter-offer? Does she recommend going to trial because you have a strong case, despite his rejection of the offer? Now, go and do something that's relaxing and rejuvenating. Take a walk, do some yoga, read a trashy romance novel, if that's your thing. Once you've done what you can, there's no point in living in the upset anymore.

Emotional invincibility is not about stuffing your emotions or denying them. It's not about becoming an emotionless robot. If you attempt to stuff your emotions and deny them expression, they'll get stuck. Then, when the slightest upset happens (oftentimes completely unrelated to the original upset you ignored), they'll pop out and cause a scene. Trust me, you don't want that! The goal is to allow the emotions to move through your body efficiently so they can be released, and you can get on with life. It's best not to have important conversations or make major decisions when you're overly emotional. Wait until emotions subside, and then decide or have the discussion.

It's been several years since I learned the principles of developing emotional invincibility. It's rare that something gets me emotionally upset, and I don't even need to set my phone timer anymore! It's just a blip on my emotional radar. I take a deep breath when I feel the upset rising in me, and then I breathe it out. I say to myself, "I can't change this, so I refuse to be upset about it. How can I make the best of this situation?" Trust me, it takes lots of practice on the little things before you become unflappable for the big things.

QUESTIONS TO CONSIDER & ACTION ITEMS:

Stop fighting your emotions; get curious about them instead.

Can you name the root cause of the emotion?

Give your emotions room. Feel them and let them pass through your body.

Wait until your emotions have subsided before interacting with your money.

Start practicing the emotional invincibility technique when you feel overwhelmed with emotion.

Chapter 23

DREAMING OF A BETTER FUTURE

*I*t's perfectly okay, and even necessary, to start dreaming of a better financial future, even when things are still a mess. When you watch your former life crash and burn before your eyes, it's easy to become hopeless or even depressed. That's why holding a Dream Session is so important. Like the phoenix who is consumed by the fire and rises from the ashes, there is an abundant life for you after divorce.

The first step is to answer the following question: *"If I woke up tomorrow and felt REALLY good about my financial situation, what would that look like?"* The answer is different for everyone, so don't worry about your answers being "right" or "wrong." Here are answers I hear from divorcing women on a regular basis:

- "My credit cards are paid in full."
- "I have the cash to go on vacation and not stress out over the cost."
- "My kids have money in their college funds."

- "My student loans are gone."
- "I'm confident about my financial future."
- "I have money set aside for emergencies and opportunities."

In order to flesh out the details of what your Preferred Financial Future looks like, here are some additional questions to ask:

- What do I want to HAVE?
- What do I want to DO?
- Where do I want to GO?
- What do I want to GIVE?
- Who do I want to BE?

Don't put limits on your dreams and goals during this session. Don't worry about *how* you're going to accomplish them right now. Come up with some dreams and goals you get excited about achieving, even if they seem absurd, frivolous, or impossible.

The second step in the Dream Session is creating your Financial Vision Board. Which dreams excite you the most? A vision board is simply a physical representation and reminder of those dreams. Search the internet and magazines for pictures that represent your dreams. Grab a glass of wine, print or cut out those pictures, and put them on a poster board or bulletin board. It can be as fancy or as simple as you want it to be.

Hang your vision board where you'll see it daily. Create a digital vision board by having those same pictures as your wallpaper or screensaver on your computer, tablet, or phone. You might want to bring your kids into the process and have them create their own vision boards to hang in their rooms.

Don't limit yourself to a two-dimensional vision board. Some of my goals and visions are in 3-D! For example, when I wrote my first book, *Money Is Emotional*, I created a 3-D representation of it. When I settled on the title of the book, I mocked up a full-color book cover. I printed it out and taped it to a random volume from my bookshelf. Seeing "my book" on my desk motivated me to keep writing and make it a reality. If there's a certain car you dream of owning, get a miniature version of it and put it on your desk or night stand.

Pair your Magnetic Money Mantras™ with your vision board pictures! Use a photo editing website like Canva to write your affirmations ON your vision board pictures. For example, while writing the first draft of this book, I had a picture of a red Alfa Romeo Giulia on my phone's home screen with the caption, "I'm the proud owner of a brand new, paid in full, Alfa Romeo!" It was my screen saver for seven months, until I bought it with cash! It ended up being a white car with red interior, but I actually liked it better than the red one! And here's the crazy thing…I didn't even test drive it until three days before I bought it! This is why it's important to see the goals and dreams you're working toward: It keeps your motivation high. Your vision boards – both physical and digital – will serve as a positive fuel to propel you toward a better future.

Most women I know, especially mothers, have a giving, self-sacrificing nature. So this whole exercise might feel weird and even wrong for you. You've spent so many years catering to others – your ex, your children, your church, your friends, and your boss – that you have stopped wanting things for yourself. Or maybe you never even started.

It's not wrong to want things for yourself – and yourself alone. You are not selfish or greedy. Divorcing women who are coming out of codependent or narcissistic relationships have an especially hard time with this because they've pushed their needs, preferences, and wants down for so long, they honestly don't know what they want.

Shortly after I broke up with Jeff, my counselor, Dave, asked me a seemingly simple question during one of our sessions, "What's your favorite ice cream, Christine?"

"Cookies and cream," I replied.

"Was that Jeff's favorite ice cream?" my counselor asked.

"Yeah, so?" I replied.

"You don't even know what your favorite ice cream is!" Dave declared.

As I was leaving the session, Dave gave me a homework assignment: go to the grocery store, buy five different pints of ice cream that looked delicious, and decide on my favorite ice cream. (It's Ben & Jerry's Mint Chocolate Cookie, in case you're wondering.)

This isn't an uncommon occurrence. A few years ago, I conducted a Dream Session with my divorcing client, Mindy, mother of six. We knew she would soon receive a sizable settlement, which was a relief. When I asked her what sorts of things and experiences she wanted on the other side of divorce, she had her list. She wanted at least one family vacation per year. She wanted to help with her children's college. She wanted to work part-time so she could babysit her first grandchild.

I interrupted her list, and asked, "Mindy, what do you want just for YOU?" She got very quiet and then burst into tears. "Hey," I said softly, "tell me what's going on." She said through her tears, "No one's ever asked me that."

Maybe no one's ever asked you that question either. Woman to woman, let me tell you: *It's more than okay to want things for yourself and no one else!* It's also okay to not know what you want or prefer right at this moment. But allow yourself to dream, to stretch, to consider, and to test-drive and figure out your preferences.

QUESTIONS TO CONSIDER & ACTION ITEMS:

Conduct your Dream Session and answer the following questions:

What do you want to DO?

What do you want to HAVE?

Where do you want to GO?

What do you want GIVE?
Who do you want to BE?
Create your financial vision board.

Chapter 24

MAGNETIC MONEY MANTRAS™

ere's a vital fact you need to know: The conscious part of your brain controls only about 5% of your daily actions! Your unconscious brain controls the other 95% of your behavior. "How am I supposed to change my behavior if the conscious part of my brain only controls 5% of my actions?" you ask. The wonderful news is you can utilize your conscious mind to *choose* the thoughts you want to believe. Then you systematically impress them onto your unconscious mind through repetition.

What's the answer to ridding your brain of negative money thoughts? We can control what we think. The first step is to identify your negative money thoughts, which you did in a previous chapter. You then need to reprogram the nonconscious part of your brain by replacing the negative with positive, productive money thoughts. These will, with time, change the emotions you feel around money, making forward progress seem easy and even fun.

You can't just say, "Okay, from this point forward, I'm not going to think about those negative things. I'm not going to believe them anymore." Nature abhors a vacuum, so you have to crowd out the negative statements with positive money mantras.

Your unconscious mind wants you to agree with yourself. Once you start repeating these Magnetic Money Mantras™, it's very hard for your unconscious mind to hold two opposing thoughts at the same time. At first, your unconscious mind is going to resist, and it's going to want to hold on to the old, negative thoughts. Those thoughts are comfortable and familiar, even though they're not serving you anymore. That's why you need to repeat (and repeat, and repeat) your new, better mantras to embed them down into your unconscious mind and overwrite those negative ones.

Let's look at how you can take your list of negative money thoughts and turn them into positives!

For example:

- Instead of saying, "That's too expensive," you can replace it with "Of course, I can afford to buy the things I need and want."
- Instead of saying, "I'll never pay off my student loans," you can replace this with "It's normal for me to pay extra on my student loans every month, and they're disappearing before my eyes."
- Instead of saying, "I'll never make enough money to support myself," you can replace it with, "I'm the kind of woman who earns an amazing salary with plenty of money to pay the bills and enjoy life."
- Instead of saying, "I don't understand investing," you can replace this with, "I am a capable and educated investor."

Maybe you created money affirmations or mantras in the past, and they didn't work for you, despite repeating them over and over and over again. There's a specific formula for ensuring your money mantras are effective and magnetic so they attract more abundance into your life. Your mantras should be positive, present-tense, specific, action and results oriented, and most importantly, pass the "Hell Yes Test."

First, your new money mantras must be 100% positive. Leave out any words with a negative connotation or energy for you. My client, LeeAnn, came up with this mantra for herself: "I'm financially free from my ex-husband." I loved the sentiment, but the word "ex-husband" is negative. Plus, she didn't feel good saying this mantra over and over again thanks to the word "ex-husband." So we improved it to: "I'm a financially independent woman!" Everything about this new mantra is positive, and it makes LeeAnn feel amazing every time she says it. Avoid any negative words or phrases, especially anything you personally have a negative gut reaction to, and find a better way to phrase it. When composing your money mantras, avoid double negatives. You might think they cancel each other out, but they don't in your unconscious mind. For example, don't say, *"I never bounce any checks."* Instead declare, *"There's always plenty of money in my checking account."*

You don't want ANY negative language in your Magnetic Money Mantras™!

The second step is to phrase your money mantras in the present tense, **not the future tense.** Your unconscious mind operates in the present. If you say, "I will have an emergency fund of $50,000," your unconscious brain responds, "Oh, that's in the future, so I don't need to worry about it." But if you say, "I'm so happy and grateful I have $50,000 in my savings account," you're saying it's occurring right now, in the present. If it hasn't happened yet, your unconscious mind responds with, "Hmm, if this is supposed to be my reality, maybe I need to do something to make sure this happens!" Stating your mantras in the present prompts you to take action and not procrastinate.

Step number three is to include very specific details to amplify positive emotion. So, rather than saying, "I'm always taking beach vacations," it would be better to say, "I'm the kind of woman who spends at least one month, every year on the Island of Maui." It's hard to get excited about vague ideas. Plus, if you say "I'm always taking beach vacations," you might get an offer to go to the Jersey shore for a weekend instead of Maui for a month, which is what you really want. If you want to use the power of your unconscious mind, you need to "order" exactly what you want to be delivered.

Step four is to incorporate action and results into your money mantras whenever possible. Rather than saying, "I'm a wealthy and generous woman," (which is still a good thing to say), it would be better to say, "Of course I carry around hundred-dollar bills to bless strangers with as I feel led!" This is inferring you've achieved a level of financial success that allows you to carry around $100 bills for the sole purpose of giving to a homeless person or blessing a friend who's going through a hard time. So any time you're able to work in action and specific results, you absolutely want to do it.

The fifth and final step for your Magnetic Money Mantras™ is to pass the "Hell Yes Test." When you say your money mantra out loud, how does it make you feel? Does it make you feel excited? Does it make you feel happy? It might even make you feel a little nervous, but as long as it's a positive, excited kind of nervous, then that's okay. You don't want it to feel heavy. stressful, or worse, boring. You want to say your mantra and immediately feel like, "Hell yes! This is happening!" Passing the "Hell Yes Test" is the most important of the five steps.

ACTION ITEM:

Take your list of the ten negative things you think or say about money and rewrite them as positives.

Be sure to incorporate the Five Steps for Magnetic Money Mantras™:

Positive

Present Tense

Specific

Action & Results Oriented

Passes the "Hell Yes Test"

Chapter 25

WAYS TO PHRASE YOUR MONEY MANTRAS

Because we're unique individuals, the same exact mantra might not resonate and pass the "Hell Yes Test" for every divorcing woman. My goal is to give you options to craft your own Magnetic Money Mantras™ that feel amazing to you. Over the years, I've collected and tested a variety of ways to phrase your money mantras, several of which I learned from my amazing business and mindset coach, Jenna Faith.

I want you to experiment and find the ones that flow naturally for you. If you phrase your mantra a certain way and it doesn't pass the "Hell Yes Test," modify or scrap it. Personally, I like to mix things up so I don't get bored; I don't want all of my mantras to sound exactly the same.

The first type of money mantra is "claiming." You're claiming something for yourself, as if it's already yours. There are three variations of the claiming mantra: I am, I have, and I choose.

Here are some examples of I AM mantras:

"I am a mindful spender who shops for the things I need and want with a sense of peace and satisfaction."

"I am an excellent saver! I love depositing 10% of everything I earn into my savings account."

Here are some examples of I HAVE mantras:

"I have an abundance fund to help and bless people with, as I feel led."

"I have more than $50,000 in the bank."

Here are some examples of I CHOOSE mantras:

"I choose to earn an amazing income doing what I love and what comes easily for me."

"I choose to manage my money wisely."

The second way to phrase money mantras is "normalizing." You're taking the things you want and stating them as if it is normal for you to be this way and to have these things. You are bringing them into your comfort zone. Think about which of your mantras you want to be a normal part of your everyday life.

The first one is simply, IT'S NORMAL FOR ME TO…

"It's normal for me to receive passive income of $5,000 or more each and every month."

"It's normal for me to pay cash for a new car."

You can also say, "I'M THE KIND OF WOMAN WHO…

"I'm the kind of successful woman who has a personal chef and a cleaning lady."

"I'm the kind of woman who receives regular raises and promotions at my job, even when no one else does!"

Another one that we can use to normalize is EVER SINCE. This is acting as if our mantra has already happened. Yes, I told you to make your mantras present tense, but you can also state them in past tense as if it's already happened. This makes your unconscious mind say, "Whoa, what did I miss? I better catch up!"

Here's an example: "Ever since I paid off my credit card debt, I'm putting $700 extra per month toward a Disney vacation for my family." The goal is having the credit card paid off so you can take a Disney vacation. And you're basically saying it's a done deal, right?

Another normalizing mantra phrase to use is OF COURSE.

"Of course, I use debt wisely and in moderation to buy things of lasting value."

"Of course, I drive an Alfa Romeo Giulia paid for with cash." Of course, this is the kind of life you have!

Another one of the ways to phrase mantras is "energizing." Energizing mantras express happiness, joy, and excitement. But at the same time, they also express thankfulness and gratitude. The gratitude magnifies and compounds the original emotion (happiness), which makes this way to phrase very powerful. The basic formula is: I'M SO HAPPY AND GRATEFUL... Personally, I like to mix it up, so sometimes I say, "I'm so excited and thankful" or "I'm excited and delighted."

Here are some examples: "I'm so excited and grateful I spent every January in a luxury beachfront hotel on the island of Maui."

"I'm so happy and thankful I just accepted my dream job with company XYZ, making double my former salary!"

"I'm so excited and delighted that my business is consistently making consistent $10k months!"

I highly recommend you use some energizing money mantras!

What happens when your inner critic is rearing its ugly head, despite your positive money mantras? When you say something positive and it's not true yet, your inner critic wakes up. If you say, "I am a six-figure business owner" (and it's not true yet), the little negative voice in your head will say, *"No, you're not!"* So, how do you overcome your inner critic and turn it off?

Here are two critic-busting techniques to use. The first one is I'M IN THE PROCESS OF...., as in, "I'm in the process of becoming a six-figure income earner." Even if you're not there yet, using "I'm in the process of" cancels out your inner critic's argument. Because you can say, "Well, yes, I am. I'm improving each and every day; I'm learning new things. I might not be there yet, but I AM in the process of becoming a six-figure business owner."

Another inner-critic busting technique I love is known as Afformations®, created by Noah St. John and detailed in his book *The Little Book of Afformations®*. Rather than stating your mantra, you use a *why* question instead. This unplugs your inner critic and simultaneously activates your unconscious mind to go to work on your behalf. It works because your inner critic can't respond "no" to a why question. Also, why questions naturally cultivate curiosity. I love using Afformations®, especially for areas where my inner critic is very strong.

You: "Why am I a capable and educated investor?"
Inner Critic: "Um…" (silence)

Here's the reason your critic is silent: because you can't argue with a why question. A why question activates your unconscious mind to search for an answer, not start an argument.

"Hmm, why am I a capable and educated investor? Maybe I took a class on investing basics and started subscribing to the Wall Street Journal. I found and hired a wonderful financial planner who explains my investment choices to me and guides me to make wise financial decisions." If you find your inner critic is rearing its ugly head, try turning your mantras into Afformations®, by phrasing them as why questions.

What happens if you create your Magnetic Money Mantras™ exactly as I prescribed, but you still feel resistance, anxiety, or doubt when you say them? It could be that you are trying too hard and stretching too far. Let's say your current reality is that you and your three small children are living with your parents. Because you scraped together all your money to hire an attorney to divorce your abusive husband, your bank account is in danger of going negative on a daily basis.

Saying a mantra like, "Of course, I have $50,000 in the bank," might not make you feel good right now because it seems impossible from your current vantage point. The mantra itself is good and positive, but it doesn't make you feel good or positive. It makes you feel like a failure, so it definitely doesn't pass the "Hell Yes Test."

Because you always want the emotions around your Magnetic Money Mantras™ to be positively charged, it's time to employ "bridge mantras." When there's a HUGE gap in between your current reality and the goal you desire, it can cause us anxiety. You might need to create a bridge mantra (or two or three) to help you navigate the gap with positivity. Let's look at how bridge mantras take you from this current reality to your ultimate goal.

Current Reality: My bank account balance is so low; I'm terrified I'm going to get overdraft fees.

Bridge Mantra 1: Of course, my bank balance is always positive and my bills are paid. I'm going to be okay.

Bridge Mantra 2: It's normal for me to have a minimum balance of $1,000 in my bank account, and $200 a month in fun money.

Bridge Mantra 3: I'm the kind of woman who buys the things I need and want with a sense of peace and satisfaction, because I have an extra $10,000 in the bank.

Ultimate Reality: Of course, I have a minimum of $50,000 in the bank!

As my coach and mentor, Melanie Ann Layer, says, "What is the better feeling thought?" Use one or more bridge mantras over time to get yourself to the ultimate mantra you want to achieve. It's all about taking steps in the right direction!

It takes time to overwrite your negative money self-talk, just as it takes time for an acorn to grow into an oak tree. Repetition is the key to impressing these positive mantras on your unconscious mind, which will crowd out and replace the negative thoughts.

ACTION ITEMS:

Take your list of money mantras from the previous chapter. Incorporate the various "ways to phrase" that appeal to you.

Once you have your list of Magnetic Money Mantras™, repeat them out loud daily, until you have them memorized. If you enjoy journaling, I encourage you to write out your top ten Magnetic Money Mantras™ daily.

Chapter 26

RESPECT YOUR MONEY

One of the keys to a great relationship with anyone is respect. Respect means you value, honor, and show courtesy to someone or something. When another person disrespects you, you want to get away from them as soon as possible!

You are in a relationship with money, and you're going to be together forever. *Do you respect your money?* Do you value and honor your money? If you don't, money will always flee from you. If you're wondering why money goes right back out as soon as it comes in, it might be your lack of respect for it.

Here are some signs you're disrespecting your money:

- Your cash is disorganized and wadded up.
- You have loose change accumulating in random parts of your house and car.

- You have torn and crumpled receipts all over the place.
- Your bills and other financial papers are disorganized.
- Your wallet or purse is threadbare and falling apart.
- You continue to think and say negative things about money.

Respecting money is both an energetic and a physical practice. Changing the way you think and talk about money is an essential first step, but it doesn't stop there. When you physically handle cash, respect it. Don't wad it up and treat your cash like trash! Ensure your bills are neatly folded in your wallet. Designate spots for spare change in your home and car, and deposit it in your bank accounts regularly.

Give your money a good home. If your purse or wallet is worn out, permission granted to buy a new (reasonably priced) one. Use a pretty container like a flowered tea cup or even a cute piggy bank for your coins. Are you giving your money room to grow? If you have no savings, open a savings account. If you have no investments, open an investment account! Your money needs a place to go, and you can start these accounts with a very small amount. No need to wait until you have $1,000!

You don't need an intricate filing system for your financial paperwork, business or personal. In fact, many people keep way more financial paperwork than necessary. Because of online banking, you can easily access your monthly statements, copies of checks, and payment histories. There's no need to drown in piles of paper clutter!

Designate a spot in your house for unpaid bills. As soon as the mail comes in, open the bills and put them in their rightful place. I always sort my bills so the one that's due first is right on top. I can tell with a glance when I need to mail a check or pay the bill online. Paying bills late because you're disorganized can cost you in late fees and potential dings on your credit.

I only keep one month's history of utility bills. When I pay this month's bill, I check to ensure last month's payment is reflected. Then I shred the paid bill from the prior month. I have a few file folders for tax-related paperwork: current year donations, H.S.A. receipts, and estimated tax payments (since I'm self-employed).

If you're self-employed and run a business, you will need additional files for your receipts, financial statements, and invoices. Don't be like my artist friend who used to accumulate her business receipts and tax paperwork in a trash bag she kept in her closet! At the very least, get 12 folders and write the months of the year on each one. Put your receipts and bank statements in the appropriate month's folder. This will make tax time a much more relaxing experience! I prefer to buy file folders with beautiful designs that make me smile every time I see them. My money doesn't want to live in a plain manilla home, and it only costs a few extra bucks at the office supply store.

I know it seems strange to think that your money wants to be respected and cared for, but it does. And it responds positively when you do. My clients always experience financial increase when they begin to respect their money.

QUESTIONS TO CONSIDER:

In what ways am I disrespecting my money?
How am I going to show my money respect going forward?
What do I need to do to give my money a good home?

Chapter 27

SPENDING QUALITY TIME WITH MONEY

ow much positive attention do you give your personal finances on a weekly and monthly basis? Are you only interacting with your finances when it's absolutely required? In addition to respecting your money, you must spend quality time with it on a regular basis.

Here are some signs you are neglecting your money:

- You frequently pay bills late.
- You lose or misplace bills and other financial paperwork.
- You've had multiple overdraft fees within the last six months.
- You don't know how much money is in your accounts.
- You're always unpleasantly surprised when quarterly or annual bills come due.

- Your credit score isn't good and you have multiple blemishes on your credit report.

Don't worry; spending quality time with your finances doesn't mean you have to spend an hour a day pouring over multi-tab spreadsheets. I recommend you schedule a weekly recurring "Date Night" with money in your calendar. No, it doesn't have to occur at 8 PM on a Saturday night. It can be any day of the week or time of the day. I conduct my weekly money dates on Saturday mornings around 10 AM. Schedule yours when you will be calm, alert, and uninterrupted. For you, it might be 10 PM on a Tuesday when the kids are in bed. Once you get into the habit of doing this weekly, your money date should only take you about 20 minutes or so.

What should you do during your money date? First, check your actual spending versus your plan. Which categories are on track? Which are over or under budget? Do you need to modify your plan to shift money from one category to another?

I recommend tracking your spending electronically to stay on top of your progress. Once you set up a personal finance app, it saves so much time and effort than manually updating spreadsheets or Google Docs. (Unless you love that sort of thing!) Plus, you can check your spending in real time to make better decisions. Personal finance apps pull all of your spending transactions into one place, which is helpful when you have multiple bank accounts and credit cards. There are plenty of free and low-cost options available. Your bank might already have a budget function built into your online banking.

The second thing you'll do during your money date is pay any bills due within the next 7 to 10 days. This weekly rhythm ensures you're not overlooking a bill and paying it late. If you're a disorganized or fly-by-the-seat-of-your-pants bill payer, you risk missing due dates and incurring late fees. It might not seem like a big deal to pay an extra $5 here or $20 there, but over the long term, it can add up to big bucks!

Finally, if you don't have automatic transfers set up to your savings and investment accounts, do this during your weekly money date. If you're self-employed, this is also the time to pay yourself and transfer money into a savings account for your estimated quarterly tax payments.

A relatively small amount of quality time spent on your personal finances pays big dividends. Your money wants to be managed properly; it doesn't want to be ignored!

QUESTIONS TO CONSIDER & ACTION ITEMS:

In what ways have you been neglecting your money?

What day and time each week will you have your "Date Night" with money?

Go put it on your calendar as a recurring appointment NOW.

Chapter 28

REWRITE YOUR LETTER TO MONEY

emember the letter you wrote to money? Take it out and read it again. Are you committed to changing your relationship with money? If so, you'll need to consistently think and speak well of money, in addition to giving it a good home and spending quality time with it.

I want you to rewrite your letter to money as if it were one year in the future. Imagine the best possible outcome has occurred for you and money. Answer the following questions in your letter as you address money:

- What does your financial life look like right now?
- How do you feel about your money?
- What has changed?
- How are things better?

If you want, you can take your first letter and rewrite it in positive terms, sentence by sentence. The more specific and emotionally charged this letter is, the better.

The first step to a better relationship with money is imagining that it is possible!

Let's look at my letter to money from Chapter 13. Here's the "before" version, in case you forgot what it said.

Dear Money,

I am SO sorry for all the ways I let you down and mistreated you over the past seven years. I allowed Jeff to talk me into spending you on his alcohol and weed. I let him borrow you to bail him out of both his money messes and his legal messes, rather than keep you safe in the bank. I know you wanted to protect me and take care of me. But I dragged you into seedy situations like bounced checks, pawn shops, and payday loans. I didn't stand up for us, but allowed Jeff to mistreat us both. I'm sorry I didn't leave sooner.

And most of the time, I blamed you. There wasn't enough of you to go around to pay the bills. If I just had more of you, then life would be okay. The truth is, more of you would have only magnified and prolonged the problem. I have lots of regrets about how I have treated you in the past, Money. I promise, I am going to do everything I can to make it up to you. So please stay with me and let me try again.

~ Christine

Obviously, I have an advantage, because I know exactly what my financial life looked like a year after leaving Jeff. Honestly things turned out even better than I could have imagined! Here's my "after" letter.

Dear Money,

The past year has seen SO many exciting and positive changes for us! Yes, it's taken effort to get us organized and start rebuilding good financial habits. Dad helped us create a solid plan to continue with our progress. We now have thousands of dollars in savings, and all of our bills are caught up. No more collector calls! Our credit score is steadily improving. I love that we spend time together every week reviewing our results and planning for our future. And speaking of the future...we're now dating Nick, who is a wonderful example of how to wisely manage money. I know he will treat both of us well in this relationship.

Because I respect you, more of you is flowing into my life! I just received a raise at work, and I don't think it's any coincidence. I also have an opportunity to sell my old truck and buy a nice new-to-me Honda Accord for a very affordable price. Things are looking up for us, Money! And I have a feeling they're only going to get better.

~ Christine

ACTION ITEM:

It's your turn! Rewrite your letter to money as if it were one year in the future. Imagine the best possible outcome has occurred for you and money. Read your positive letter to money out loud every day for the next 30 days.

Part Five

MANAGING YOUR MONEY

Chapter 29

ASSESSING YOUR MONEY SITUATION

*M*ost women feel some level of financial anxiety during and after divorce. The cure for this anxiety isn't to avoid looking at your money situation. Yet, that's exactly what many divorcing women do! They constantly worry about money and even work themselves to panic attacks. The only way to effectively combat financial anxiety is to assess the state of your finances. Then and only then can you take constructive action to make things better.

Melissa Joy, CFP®, CDFA®, says, "It's important to make a money plan before and during your divorce. Don't wait until after you have a settlement to bring a financial professional into the conversation. Also, you should consider avoiding big money decisions during the transition period if at all possible."

The first step is to gather as much information as you can about your income, expenses, assets (what you own), and debts (what you owe.) If you're mid-divorce and a settlement hasn't been reached yet, you'll need to create an interim plan, based on your current income and expenses. I find that women use the excuse of "the divorce isn't final, so I can't create a plan yet," to procrastinate on this important step. However, most states will require you to provide this information on your assets, debts, income, and spending as part of the divorce process anyway.

I call this honest assessment of your starting point the "Reality Check." The goal of this exercise isn't to change anything (yet). Your objective here is to record and report the facts of your financial situation, not to judge yourself. Approach the Reality Check like a detective or archeologist on a discovery mission. You can even pretend you're looking at someone else's financial information, which helps remove the emotional zing.

Schedule your Reality Check for a time when you'll be calm, focused, and uninterrupted. If math and numbers are not your strong suit, you might want to enlist the help of a financial coach or money-smart friend to assist you with this step. Most people need one to two hours to complete this process. I encourage you to schedule a time within the next three days to conduct your Reality Check.

Here are the items you will need:

- Monthly household bills: mortgage/rent payment, utilities (electric, cell phone, water, internet and streaming services), car insurance, etc.
- Credit card statements: monthly minimums and payoffs
- Other debt payments: car payments, medical bills, home equity line of credit, student loans. monthly minimums and payoffs for all
- Amounts spent monthly on: gas, groceries, eating out, entertainment, clothes, pet care, health and beauty, kid expenses (school supplies, sports, and activities)
- Pen/pencil and paper, or your laptop

Record what you have been spending per month for all of the categories above. (You may have additional spending categories not included in the list.) Total up the amount of debt you currently owe and the assets you own.

"I wish I'd had a clearer head and focused on the future," says Lisa Schnitzer, Divorce Concierge. "I wish I'd known how to plan and be strategic about money issues. It's your future, and your money needs to have attention so you can make the best decisions going forward. Get all the facts about your money. Know what you have, where it's located, and how it works for you."

Be prepared to encounter surprises during your Reality Check, both pleasant and unpleasant. You might discover you have more or less debt, cash, or assets than you thought. This step needs to be completed before you can create your Personalized Prosperity Plan. You need to know both where you're starting from and where you want to go in order to create a plan that will get you there!

Now here is the big question: *Is your current spending in line with your values, dreams, and goals?*

ACTION ITEM:

Conduct your financial Reality Check within the next 48 hours. Don't skip this!

Chapter 30

YOUR PERSONALIZED PROSPERITY PLAN

ow that you've assessed your situation, you might be thinking that I want you to create a budget to manage your money, but you'd be wrong. I want you to create a Personalized Prosperity Plan instead! Why? A Prosperity Plan is so much more than a budget, which is simply a spending plan. Budgets don't usually incorporate saving, investing, debt reduction, and income optimization. All of these are vital parts of your financial health, along with managing your spending.

Traditional budgets are restrictive and rigid, like a keto diet for your money. I don't know about you, but when I hear the words "budget" and "diet," I cringe. For most women, budgeting conjures up thoughts of deprivation, discipline, and drudgery. I don't want you to feel that way about your money! Budgets are like crash diets; you can't stay on one forever. At some point, you're going to want to loosen up and have a little fun.

Traditional budgets are frequently a "cookie cutter" plan that worked for the money guru who's touting it. They'll give you formulas and percentages for how you should be spending your money every month. The problem? The person who created the budget plan might have a completely different life and family situation from you! Let's say a financial pro says your food budget should be 10% of your after-tax income. What if you have five kids, three of whom are teenage boys? That might not be enough! If you're single and don't have any kids in the house, 10% might be too much. Trying to force yourself into a money mold that doesn't fit is going to feel miserable and awkward.

Rather than being restrictive and rigid, your Personalized Prosperity Plan is expansive and flexible. It's so much more than your income minus your spending, like a traditional budget. It has four main parts: your spending plan, your income optimization plan, your saving and investing plan, and your debt reduction plan. Most importantly, it is personalized to your situation, your dreams, and your goals. A Prosperity Plan is like a healthy eating plan you can live with. There's room for portion-controlled fun! In this section, you'll discover the various parts of the Prosperity Plan and how they fit together.

Chapter 31

MASTER YOUR SPENDING

The Spending Plan portion of your Prosperity Plan is what most money gurus refer to as the personal budget. However, I'm not a fan of the word "budget," because we liken it to a crash diet that's gluten free, sugar free, and fun free. (Yuck!) The Spending Plan balances your needs and wants, so this isn't about deprivation. I want this to be a plan you can live with for the long haul!

Mastering your spending takes priority because it's difficult to pay down debt or build up savings if your spending is out of control. Take a look at the results of your Reality Check. Where is your money being spent? Is this in line with the values and goals you established in your Dream Session? Are there categories where you're spending more than you'd like?

When I discuss spending changes with my clients, we determine where we can redirect money away from things of little importance and toward their top priorities. I don't want you to "cut your spending to the bone," in any category. Remember this is a healthy spending plan you can live with, not a beans-and-rice restrictive budget! Please don't be overly aggressive with your spending changes, because it can backfire on you.

For example, most of my clients are overspending on groceries and eating out when we first start working together. Food is a common blackhole in many people's Spending Plans. Susan, whom I coached several years ago, regularly spent $500 a month eating out. She had three teenagers and spent a good chunk of her time running them around to sports and other activities. When I showed Susan how much of her spending went to restaurants (much of it fast food), she immediately wanted to cut it in half. I encouraged her to set a more reasonable goal of reducing dining out by $100 over the next 30 days, making the goal to spend $400 instead of her usual $500. When we examined her spending a month later, Susan discovered, to her delight, that she only spent $350 instead of $500. If she had set a goal of only spending $250, Susan probably would have beaten herself up by missing the goal by $100, rather than celebrating the fact that she spent $150 less than usual!

Begin using a personal finance app or your online banking budget feature to track your spending in real time. These tools help you to make better decisions in the moment. If there are certain categories that are temptations for you, you have a few options. If possible, switch them to cash. Paying with cash literally registers as pain in your brain, which causes you to think twice about your spending. If you're not a fan of cash, put your discretionary spending money on a separate debit card. When you get paid, transfer a set amount of money to the card, and don't use any other payment method for those fun purchases. You're essentially applying portion control to your spending.

In about half of my divorcing clients, I see fear (even abject terror) around spending money, which isn't healthy either. Sometimes this fear of spending is due to a lack of clarity regarding their financial health. "Is it okay for me to spend this money? Should I be saving this for something else?" Because of uncertainty, a woman might spend very little money for fear of making a mistake. Other times the fear of spending has been conditioned into her by her ex-husband. This was the case for my client, and author, Allison K. Dagney. Her husband scrutinized every single penny she spent, despite their household income being multiple six-figures. Even though her ex no longer looked over her shoulder, she was still being cheap with herself out of habit.

So when is it okay to splurge? Some women get so entrenched in the mindset of paying down debt and saving money that they struggle with figuring out when it's okay to loosen up a little and enjoy some of their money. There is definitely a right way and wrong way to splurge, so you don't ruin your financial health.

You might think that putting splurges on hold while you're getting financially healthy is the right thing to do. Unfortunately, it can put you in danger of burning out. The journey to financial wellness is a marathon, not a sprint. This is why it is important to treat yourself and your family occasionally, even while you are in the process of saving money and paying down debt. Let's first discuss when it is *not* okay to splurge!

- It's not okay to splurge if you are in foreclosure on your house, behind on your rent or car payment, or past due on any of your bills.
- It's not okay to splurge if you don't have the cash in the bank to pay for it. Never charge your splurges on a credit card (unless you have the cash to pay it off in full at the end of the month).
- It's not okay to splurge if you don't have at least one month of your household expenses in savings. This is your financial safety net and should be your top priority, even above paying extra on your debt.

If you have a small emergency fund, you're current on your bills, and you have the cash saved up for a splurge, what else do you need to consider before you treat yourself?

Ask yourself, "Will this purchase bring me joy? If so, for how long?" If you're going to briefly put your financial progress on hold, make sure you are going to thoroughly enjoy your splurge and not regret it later.

For more nitty-gritty details on mastering your spending, grab a copy of my book *Money Is Emotional: Prevent Your Heart from Hijacking Your Wallet.*

IF SHE CAN DO IT, YOU CAN DO IT:

Krystle Atkins, Divorced Woman and CDFA®

"When I filed for divorce, my bank account was basically down to nothing. I made a very strict budget, watching every single penny, to make certain I was going to make it. I planned out several months and what-if scenarios to make sure I was going to succeed. In between the planning I cried...lots of tears. And then I cried some more. I had lots of anxiety and stress, but I stayed determined. I wasn't going to let this beat me.

I gained full control over my finances and knew exactly where money was going. I developed strategies for building up my emergency fund and paying off my student loans. I finally felt empowered! This experience eventually led me to become a financial planner so I could help other women succeed with money after divorce."

ACTION ITEMS & QUESTIONS TO CONSIDER:

Schedule a day and time to formulate your first Spending Plan.

Which tool are you going to use to track your spending?

What will be your biggest obstacle to sticking to your Spending Plan?

What can you do now to avoid or overcome that obstacle?

Chapter 32

OPTIMIZE YOUR INCOME

A s part of your Personalized Prosperity Plan, you'll need to consider how much income you need to meet your financial goals for the future. Most money gurus spend all their time discussing spending and how to cut back, while ignoring the other side of the equation: income!

Now, simply earning more income won't automatically have you achieving Financial Dignity®. More money only amplifies your current financial habits and money mindset, so it's important to improve them both as you ramp up your income.

Child support and alimony (spousal maintenance) don't last forever. Please don't wait until you only have one or two years of support payments left to start thinking about how to replace that income. The sooner you make a plan and start taking action, the greater your likelihood of success. I have divorced clients who decide to finish their college degrees or start businesses while they're receiving support. It takes time and effort to ramp up new streams of income to take them from a trickle to a gush of consistent cash. Better to start when you're not relying on them to pay the bills yet.

Millionaires, on average, have seven streams of income, not just one or two! Even if you have zero desire to be a millionaire, having multiple streams of income protects you financially through diversification. If one of them dries up, yes, it will suck, but it won't ruin you financially.

Here are potential streams of income:

- Paycheck from your employer
- Spousal or child support
- Small business ownership
- Direct sales commissions
- Royalties from writing books, music, etc.
- Online courses or memberships you create
- Affiliate income
- Dividends from investments
- Rental real estate

Creating multiple streams of income allows you to build a more stable financial situation for yourself! Income streams are often classified as active versus passive. Active means you need to exert ongoing effort and time in order to keep the stream flowing. Passive means little to no work is required to keep the stream flowing, However, passive income streams do take time, effort, and sometimes even cash to establish. It's rare that an income stream is 100% active or 100% passive. Most fall on a continuum between the two.

Let's look at the income streams I shared above and see if they are active or passive. Your paycheck from your employer is 100% active. You have to show up for work if you want to get paid! Spousal or child support is 100% passive. Once it's awarded, you automatically receive it without having to do anything. Small business ownership is usually active, but it depends on what type of business you're buying into or starting.

Direct sales organizations are a wonderful blend of active and passive income. You actively sell products you already use and love to others and make a commission. When you recruit others into the organization, you typically make an additional commission on what they sell, too.

Royalties from writing books and music are passive once the item is created. I make money every month on my book sales through Amazon and Audible whether I promote them or not. (Of course, sales definitely go up whenever I promote them!)

Online courses or memberships you create are mostly passive once you create the material and set it up in a course platform. Yes, you need to spend a little time regularly reminding people of your digital products in order to keep selling them.

Affiliate income is simply being paid for recommending a product or service. I don't know about you, but when I find something I love – a book, a course, a movie – I tell everyone about it! It only takes a few minutes to see if the company offers an affiliate program. Once you sign up, you send your unique affiliate link to friends and family when you recommend it in the future. When they buy, you get paid! One month, I earned almost $2,000 by recommending just one product. (Pretty awesome, right?)

Dividends from investments are 100% passive. You're automatically paid a dividend on a regular basis. Check with your financial planner about adding dividend-paying investments to your portfolio.

Rental real estate is an excellent income stream and wealth builder if you do it right. This one takes both knowledge and work, unless you hire a management company to handle things like screening applicants, fielding tenant complaints, and handling property repairs. I have one divorced client who owns multiple rental properties that provide her a full-time income with only a handful of work hours every week. If you want more information on how to do rental real estate the right way, I highly recommend reading Mark Dolfini's book *The Time-Wealthy Investor 2.0: Your Real Estate Roadmap to Owning More, Working Less, and Creating the Life You Want.*

So when you're thinking about diversifying your income streams, consider how active or passive it will require you to be to keep the cash flowing!

Income streams are assets, right? And are all assets income streams? Not necessarily. An asset is a resource that provides present value and can be sold for cash. An income stream is a source that provides a regular stream of money to the owner.

Not all income streams are assets! If you can't sell that income stream for cash, it's not an asset. For example, your job is an income stream, but it's not an asset, because you can't sell it to someone else. Not all assets are income streams. For example, you might own your house, precious metals (gold and silver coins), and other things of value that don't provide you with monthly cash flow.

The BIG question I get asked: Aren't my retirement investments an income stream? Only if you are taking withdrawals! Yes, they're assets, but they only become an income stream when you begin to pull the cash out in retirement.

The real goldmine is collecting assets that are also income streams. Some examples I mentioned that fit the bill are rental real estate (value of the property plus rental income), business ownership (value of business if sold plus monthly sales income), and dividend-paying stocks (value of the stock plus dividend income).

IF SHE CAN DO IT, YOU CAN DO IT

Jenna Faith, business coach and best-selling author:

"Because of my divorce, I had to navigate a mountain of debt and a huge decrease in income, plus raise my 2-year-old son. During the time of the split, I was also laid off from my "decent"-paying corporate job. I decided to begin my own venture in entrepreneurship at probably the worst time. No income, no support, mountains of debt, newly divorced, and newly single parent.

I was able to pretty quickly ramp up my income as a self-employed woman. I paid off all of the debts I had and began to thrive financially. I truly don't believe I would have been able to do this if I had stayed with my ex-husband. His mindset around money (as was mine at the time) was really detrimental to acquiring any kind of wealth. I used to make $35,000 a year in a corporate environment. Now, it's not uncommon for me to make double that in one month in my business!"

QUESTIONS TO CONSIDER & ACTION ITEMS:

What income streams do you currently have?
Are they active or passive?
What potential income streams would you like to develop and nurture for the future?

Chapter 33

THE WEIGHT OF DEBT

*I*t's rare that a woman comes out of a divorce without debt of some kind. Most families, regardless of their incomes, are carrying a combination of credit card debt, car loans, mortgages, home equity loans, and student loan debt.

During your divorce settlement, part of the financial discussion will be the division of the debt. This division is usually based on income. If your ex makes twice your income, he will typically be assigned responsibility for twice the amount of marital debt.

There are exceptions to this general rule. The first is student loan debt. If you have student loans in your name, they are yours forever. The other exception is debt tied to a specific asset. If you want to keep the Audi, and there's a car loan or lease attached to it, the payment will be your responsibility.

As assets and debts are divided up during your divorce settlement, it's very important to make sure loans are refinanced and your name is removed as a responsible party for any assets that your husband is keeping. I've heard more than one horror story about ex-husbands defaulting on car loans, and the bank coming after the wife for the money because her name was never removed from the loan. Similarly, it's important for you to ensure your ex's name is removed from the titles of any assets you're keeping. If you keep the Audi, but don't remove his name from the title, he could sell it out from under you! (Yep, I've heard this story, too!)

Once the divorce settlement is final, and you know what debt you're responsible for, and how much, it's time to make a plan for it. I frequently get questions like, "Should I aim to be 100% debt-free? Is it okay to have some debt? Is all debt created equal? Are some types of debt more dangerous than others? Do I have to cut up my credit cards?"

Your debt should not stress you out emotionally or financially. Yes, it's okay to have some debt, but it should be "debt with a purpose." Many people get into debt because it's so easy to do without even thinking about it! When you buy anything, payment plans or a store credit card are included in the pitch for the item. But excessive debt is like carrying around an extra 20, 50, or 100 pounds. It makes everyday living harder and more stressful.

Pretend I handed you a 2-pound dumbbell and asked you to carry it around all day today. You put it in your purse or backpack. You can feel the weight of it, but it's not too heavy. You might even forget it's in there by the end of the day. But suppose instead that I strapped a 50-pound weight to your back and said you had to wear it the entire day. That would make even the simplest of tasks, like bending over to tie your shoe, seem nearly impossible.

That's what it's like with debt. If you're carrying a small amount relative to your income and assets, it's not a big deal. But if your amount of debt is huge, it will feel like it's crushing you. How much debt can you comfortably carry without feeling emotionally or financially stressed? This depends on the size of your financial muscles – your income and your assets – and on your emotional comfort level with debt.

No, not all debt is created equal. I prefer my clients only borrow to buy things of value such as their home, a car, ownership in a business, or a rental property. Does that mean I'm anti-credit card? No way! It's fine to use a credit card for purchases, but I'd prefer you pay the balance in full each and every month. The average interest rate for credit cards is over 15%, which means you're making the banks richer (and yourself poorer) every time you carry a balance.

Unfortunately, bankruptcy and divorce sometimes go hand-in-hand. If you and your ex are fighting over the debt and have few assets, you might be wondering if a clean start would be a good idea. Get an outside opinion to confirm if bankruptcy is your best option. Once you come out of bankruptcy court, commit to changing your underlying habits around debt so it never happens again.

For more information on the specifics of various types of debt, please reference the Living Debt Free section of my book *Money Is Emotional: Prevent Your Heart from Hijacking Your Wallet.*

QUESTIONS TO CONSIDER & ACTION ITEMS:

Make a list of your debts, including all credit cards, loans, lines of credit, and mortgages. Write down the monthly payment and the payoff for each one.

How much total debt do you have?

How much is your total monthly debt payment?

What would you do with that money every month if you were debt free?

Are you comfortable carrying around the weight of this debt?

Where can you make adjustments in your Spending Plan to free up more money to pay off your debt?

Chapter 34

LIVING DEBT FREE

hat's the best way to systematically attack your debt? It all depends on what's most emotionally motivating for you. Yes, there's a method that's the "mathematically correct" answer. But if you aren't seeing progress fast enough – in a way that motivates you - you'll probably quit in the middle.

No matter which method you pick to prioritize your debts, the overarching idea is the same. You dedicate a set dollar amount in your spending plan for debt reduction. You pay the monthly minimum due on all of your debts, except the one you're currently focusing on eliminating. You concentrate all your extra funds to paying off that debt. When one debt is paid off, you continue to dedicate the same amount every month. You will just shift the extra funds to the next debt on your list.

When I hit financial rock bottom, I used the Volcano Method of debt reduction to dig myself out. At age 26, fresh out of my dysfunctional seven-year relationship, I found myself buried in debt, with zero savings and a less-than-stellar credit score. I was no stranger to late fees and collection calls.

When I left Jeff, the financial baggage followed me. I needed a plan to attack my debt and pay it off. I knew the mathematically correct way to pay off debt is the "Avalanche Method." This involves concentrating your extra money on the debt with the highest interest rate. But…

There was one debt that I hated more than all the others: the Dillard's credit card bill. *Why?* Because when I looked at the statement after I left Jeff, something caught my eye. He charged my Valentine's Day present on the Dillard's card, and *now I was stuck paying for it!* To say that I felt royally pissed off every time I saw the Dillard's bill is an understatement! I decided to forego conventional wisdom and pay off the bill that I hated the most first. Paying it off felt like a huge victory! And it motivated me to keep going.

I didn't realize it at the time, but this is known as the Volcano Method of debt reduction. You attack whichever debt you hate the most (the one that makes you blow your top like a volcano), without worrying about interest rates or balances. The reason it's super motivating is because it brings you massive emotional relief once the bill's paid in full. And emotion is an amazing fuel to blast away debt! Once I paid off the Dillard's card, I attacked the next disdainful debt, and so on down the line, until I reached the coveted debt-free status.

The benefit of the Volcano Method is that it channels your anger into something productive. Because this method uses your emotions to your advantage, you're more likely to stick with your plan for the long haul. The disadvantage is you might end up paying more in interest than other methods. Because anger is a common emotion during divorce, I find many of my clients choose it. What if there's only one or two debts you hate, and the rest are neutral? Begin using the Volcano method for your hated debts. Then you can switch to another method after those are paid.

What are the other debt reduction methods? The other four, besides the **Volcano,** are **Avalanche, Snowball, Cash Flow,** and **Fair Share.** Let's look at each of them so you can decide which one will be the most emotionally motivating one for you.

The Avalanche Method, also known as the Highest Interest Rate Method, involves paying the minimum due on all of your bills, then concentrating extra funds on the debt with the highest interest rate. The benefit here is saving the most money in interest payments. *The downside?* If your highest interest bill has a large balance, it could take a good long while to pay it off, which might be demoralizing. If you are someone who loves saving money, this method could be the most appealing for you. You might want to track your monthly interest payments so you can see them decreasing month over month as a way to stay pumped up.

The Snowball Method pays the minimum due on all debts, except the littlest one. You attack your smallest debt with a vengeance until it's paid off. This gives you a quick victory and is perfect for people who enjoy checking things off their list. You might even be able to knock out several small debts within a month or two! It's motivating to watch your stack of bills shrink quickly. The downside is you'll pay slightly more in interest than the Avalanche Method. If you write things on your To-Do list after you've done them just to check them off, the Debt Snowball will likely be the best method for you!

The Cash Flow Method of debt reduction involves paying off the debt with the highest monthly payment first. Just like the Snowball method, you're completely ignoring interest rates, which makes most financial pros cringe. But this method can be a huge relief for women who are experiencing a cash flow crunch. I worked with a client who had only four months left on her car payment. Once paid in full, my client would have almost $500 extra every month! The car payment wasn't the smallest debt. It wasn't the debt she hated most. And it definitely wasn't the highest interest rate. But for her situation, it made sense to pay off the car. It gave her breathing room to start her emergency savings account and pay extra on her other debts.

The Fair Share Method is different from the other four in one key way: You don't focus on one debt – you focus on them all! This involves taking the extra funds you have for debt reduction and applying it proportionally to each debt. So, if your student loan represents 60% of your total debt, you would take 60% of your extra funds and pay it on the student loan. You're paying extra each month on EVERY bill instead of just one of them. This typically appeals to people with a strong sense of fairness. The downside of this method is that it involves more math (and probably a spreadsheet) to figure out. I find only a small percentage of people find this particular one appealing, but I wanted to mention it in case that's you.

Which method appeals to you and makes the most sense for your financial situation right now? Sometimes my clients will start with one method like the Cash Flow or the Volcano, then later shift to the Snowball or Avalanche. If you feel your drive to pay down debt flagging, return to this chapter and see if switching to another method rejuvenates your motivation!

QUESTIONS TO CONSIDER:

Which method of debt payoff appeals to you the most: Volcano, Snowball, Avalanche, Cash Flow, or Fair Share?

Are you ready to move toward debt-free living?

Chapter 35

SAVING FOR THE FUTURE

*M*any women find it hard to motivate themselves to save money. That's because delayed gratification goes against the grain of our very biology. Humans are hardwired to choose a sure reward today over a potentially bigger, but less certain, reward in the future. It's called "Present Bias." So how do you overcome this tendency? I'll give you a hint: It has nothing to do with discipline. But first, let's talk about the reasons you're going to want to save money.

The top three things you'll be saving for are emergencies, large purchases, and retirement (which we'll discuss in a later chapter). I'll admit that saving for emergencies isn't the most fun thing in the world. But life happens to us all, and the only thing unexpected about emergencies isn't IF they'll happen, but when. Emergency savings puts a cushion between you and life. If you have no savings and your car needs a new engine, you have both a car problem and a money problem.

And, if you prefer, you don't have to call it your "emergency fund." You can call it your Financial Freedom Fund, since it keeps you free from charging your unplanned expenses. Other possible alternatives are your Money Margin Account or your Cash Cushion Account. If you need to call it something else to help you feel good about funding it, then please do!

The goal for my clients is six months of living expenses in an easy-to-access savings or money market account. If your necessary monthly expenses (household bills, mortgage, insurance, groceries, minimum payments due on your debts) are $5,000, your emergency fund goal will be $30,000. If you currently have $0 in savings, $30k might seem impossible! That's why I'm a big fan of mini goals. Create your first goal of getting one month of your expenses in savings. Once you reach it, set the next goal for two months, and so on.

If you don't yet have a savings account, that's step zero. In order to have savings, you first need someplace for it to go! Don't be overly concerned with your rate of return on your savings account. Your emergency fund is not an investment! Sure, you can shop around for an account with .10% better interest rate, but the most important thing is to start saving now.

You might be wondering if you should concentrate on debt reduction or savings first. I advise all my clients to accumulate a mini emergency fund before paying extra on debt. I define the mini emergency fund as at least one month of your household expenses. Here's the reason why: if you have zero dollars in savings and an unexpected expense comes up, you'll end up charging it on a credit card. The mini emergency fund prevents that from happening.

Another reason you need to save money is for large purchases like vacations, cars, furniture, and Christmas gifts. If you don't save for these purchases in advance, you'll end up financing them and paying 15% or more in interest charges. Compile a list of the larger purchases you'd like to make, the approximate cost of each, and the date you plan to buy them. This will allow you to divide the cost by the number of months you have to save and establish your monthly contribution amount. If you're planning on taking a vacation in 10 months and the approximate cost is $3,000, you'll need to set aside $300 per month into a savings account to cover it. Be sure to add these monthly amounts into your spending plan!

How many savings accounts do you need? If you're traditionally employed, you'll need at least two: an emergency fund and a purchases fund. If you're self-employed, I highly recommend a third savings account for your estimated quarterly tax payments. Some of my clients like to have a savings account for each of their major goals. Others like to keep things streamlined, and use fewer accounts.

It's also helpful to remember that spending and saving are two sides of the same coin; savings is money we are spending LATER, not never! Replace "I never get to spend this money" with "I get to spend this money later!"

Because self-discipline isn't dependable, I highly recommend putting your saving and investing on autopilot. Although mindless spending is a bad thing, mindless saving is a wonderful thing! If you give yourself the choice to transfer money into your savings account every pay period, there will be times when you choose not to. However, if you set up an automatic transfer to your savings account a day after you get paid, it happens no matter what. You just need to exercise a tiny bit of willpower once, and the savings habit happens automatically. Start small, even if it's just $25 a week! Once it feels painless, you know it's time to bump up the amount. Now that you know why you should be saving money, let's talk about how to make you excited to do it!

QUESTIONS TO CONSIDER & ACTION ITEMS:

Make a list of your savings and retirement accounts and the balance in each of them. Don't have a savings account? Go online or to your local bank and open one up! Remember, your money needs a good home.

Look at your Spending Plan to determine your total monthly expenses. Based on this number, how many months of your expenses do you currently have in savings?

Do you have a mini emergency fund (one month of expenses)? If not, focus your efforts there first before paying extra on your debt.

For what purchases are you currently saving?

Are you contributing to your retirement plan? If so, how much? If not, why not?

Chapter 36

EMOTIONALLY CHARGED SAVING

*I*f you really want to ramp up your saving and investing, you need a *burning desire* to save. I'm going to show you how to use both positive and negative emotions to supercharge your desire to save with a technique I call "Emotionally Charged Saving."

As I previously mentioned, humans are hardwired to avoid pain and unpleasantness. Avoiding pain is actually a *greater* force for motivation than embracing pleasant situations. Fear is a primal and irrational emotion. Many women experience some form of fear surrounding money issues, and it can hold you back from being financially healthy. But did you know that our money fears can be harnessed to move us toward positive change?

The best way to fuel a burning desire to change our financial behavior is with *both* positive and negative emotions. Certain women (like me) are very goal-oriented and respond well to positive motivation, which is why I asked you to make a Financial

Vision Board with pictures of your money goals. Others are more motivated by avoiding negative consequences.

You've likely seen how negative emotions and experiences cause people to change their physical health. Think of the woman you know, who for years partied like a sorority girl into her 40's…that is, until she had a cancer scare. Turning on a dime, this woman is now preaching the gospel of good nutrition and running marathons on weekends. The promises of good health, better sleep, and fewer aches and pains weren't enough to motivate this woman to take care of herself. It wasn't until she was "scared straight" by a health crisis that she changed her ways. Unfortunately, many of us are this way with our finances. The good news is you can use a similar technique in the area of money, *without* having a near-fatal financial event.

With a little help from your imagination, you can produce this same powerful force to transform your finances. You see, your brain can't differentiate between *actual* events that happen to you and events you vividly imagine in your mind. The imagination is a powerful force you can use as a rocket booster to propel you toward your Preferred Financial Future. When you imagine both the positive benefit of your savings goals and the negative consequences of not achieving them, the result is Emotionally Charged Saving.

Here's an example of how I emotionally charge one of my personal financial goals. I want to retire to the island of Maui. My husband and I vacationed there twice and adore everything about the island: the beaches, the golf courses, and the perfect weather. I have pictures of the type of house we'd like to live in on our vision board. I have pictures of the beaches and golf courses on Maui. This gives me a warm fuzzy feeling whenever I see our Financial Vision Board. But is it enough to ensure I'm going to make saving and investing for retirement a priority above spending the money now?

I add fuel to the emotional fire by imagining how life in retirement will be if we *don't* achieve our savings goals. Now I'll have to remain in my current home, or even downsize to a smaller home. I won't be able to move to Maui, so I'll be facing miserable Cincinnati winters with bad driving conditions. I hate the cold and snow, so this makes me depressed because I'd much rather be sitting in the sand sipping a tropical drink with a tiny umbrella. I won't have any money to take our nieces and nephews on vacation or help with their college expenses. I might even have to go into a government-funded nursing home in my final years. (Shudder!)

I let my imagination go wild with how horrible it will be to fail at achieving the retirement I want. Several years ago, I visited a local nursing home for low-income residents, which solidified the fear of never wanting to end up there. My mother-in-law, who saved nothing for retirement, had terminal cancer and needed a long-term care facility that accepted Medicaid. While there, I took in the sights, sounds, and smells to cement the unpleasant image in my mind. Thankfully, we were able to find my mother-in-law much nicer accommodations for her final days.

By making the contrast of the upside of achieving your savings goal *and* the downside of failing to reach it as sharp as possible, you'll maximize the emotional charge. Whenever I think about contributing to my retirement account, both the joy of Maui and the fear of the terrible nursing home make it very easy for me to do the right thing! Here's the bottom line: If your savings goals are emotionally charged, you're more likely to achieve them. You must have a burning desire to save for the things that are important to you. If you're not excited about your savings goals, then you don't have a big enough reason to change your behavior.

If you are finding your money goals and vision board are not giving you the motivational traction you need to make positive changes to your personal finances, consider adding some *negative emotion* to the equation. By making the contrast of the upside of achieving your money goal and the downside of failing to reach it as sharp as possible, you'll maximize the emotional charge and achieve massive motivation. Emotionally charged saving beats discipline and willpower every time!

ACTION ITEM:

Take one of your saving or investing goals and super charge it with both positive and negative emotion. Write down the best imaginable outcome and also the worst-case scenario if you don't save the money you need to achieve your goal.

Chapter 37

INVESTING FOR RETIREMENT

The final reason to set aside money is to invest for growth. Investing is savings on steroids! You want major growth on this money to provide income in retirement. Saving and investing are similar, yet not quite the same thing. And the best way to explain it is with squirrels. *(Not what you expected, right?)*

When a squirrel stores up nuts for the winter, it's saving them to be consumed later, when food is scarce. The squirrel doesn't expect the nut to provide a harvest of additional nuts. It simply expects the food it has safely saved in its tree will be there later, in the winter, when it gets hungry. The same is true with the money in your savings accounts. You don't expect much, if any, growth. But you do expect it to be there when you need it!

You will never see a squirrel investing nuts! But if you did...here's what she would do. The squirrel would sacrifice an acorn and plant it in the ground. She would not dig the nut back up and eat it! She would be patient, knowing the acorn would eventually become an oak tree, providing hundreds, even thousands of nuts for the squirrel's children, grandchildren, and great-grandchildren. The same is true of your invested money. You plant it into your retirement accounts and keep your hands off of it for a long, long time.

Saved money should be kept in accounts that are readily available (liquid), FDIC insured, and earmarked for spending in the relatively near future. Invested money is kept inside of IRAs, 401(k)s and brokerage accounts, which are not easily accessible, have more volatility, and won't be spent for five, ten, or even twenty plus years.

Retirement statistics are pretty scary:

- According to the Department of Labor, only 46% of working women participate in a retirement plan. Part of the reason for this is that women are more likely to work part-time jobs that don't qualify for participation in a workplace retirement plan.
- According to a study by Transamerica Center for Retirement Studies, only 12% of women are "very confident" that they will be able to retire with a comfortable lifestyle.
- Just 37% of women use a professional financial advisor to help manage their retirement savings and investments.
- Only 14% of women frequently discuss saving, investing, and planning for retirement with family and close friends.
- And 25% of Americans have NO retirement savings at all!

My friend, these are statistics we need to be serious about changing! As with your savings, automating your investing is an excellent idea. If your investments are coming straight off the top of your paycheck into a 401(k) or automatically out of your checking account and into your brokerage account each month, you're more likely to invest consistently. Out of sight, out of mind! Making regular contributions over a long period of time is the recipe for retirement success.

Another way to light a fire under your backside to invest for your future is to picture your elderly self. There are websites, apps, and filters that will age a picture of "current you" to show you what you'll look like in your golden years. You might find it a little unnerving to see your elderly self, but that's the point. I hope when you look at "future you," you'll have some compassion and want to take care of her as you would your elderly parent or grandparent. Think of how you want life to be for elderly you. Do you want to be attending beachside yoga retreats or stuck in a government-funded retirement home? Print a picture of elderly you, put it on your vision board, and vow to make good investment decisions *right now*.

It's vitally important that you have a basic understanding of retirement accounts and the investments (stocks, bonds, mutual funds, ETFs) you hold in them. No, this doesn't have to become a part-time job, but you must educate yourself so you make wise investment decisions. Too many of us rely solely on our financial advisor or our company's 401(k) rep to make decisions for us. This is a bad idea because many are being paid commissions to sell you these investments. Some advisors are truly making the best decision for you and your family, but just as many are choosing the investments that best increase *their* bottom line. If you don't know enough to question their recommendations, you're in danger of being taken to the cleaners. Need a basic education on this subject? I recommend reading or listening to both *Money: Master the Game, 7 Steps to Financial Freedom* by Tony Robbins (I've read it three times!) and *Retire Inspired: It's Not an Age, It's a Financial Number* by Chris Hogan.

Here are some investing questions I'm frequently asked by my coaching clients.

Should I invest for retirement while I'm paying off debt?
Unless cash flow is super tight or your bills are behind, my answer is yes. In my opinion, you should contribute the amount needed to capture the full benefit of your employer's 401(k) match even while you're paying off debt. This is *free money* flowing into your retirement account and I don't want you to miss out on it. Even if you have no employer match, you should still be investing for retirement!

How much should I invest? Generally, you want to be investing at least 10–15% of your income for retirement. Your financial advisor will assist you with coming up with the proper amount to invest, because he or she will take into account your whole financial picture. Once your non-mortgage debt is paid in full, I recommend maxing out both your 401(k)s and IRAs. How can you tell if you're on track or behind when it comes to investing for retirement? The general rule of thumb is that you should have one times your annual income in investments by age 30, three times your income in retirement accounts by age 40, six times your income by age 50, eight times your income by age 60, and ten times your income in investments by retirement (65-70 years old).

What should I invest in? Again, a wise financial advisor will assist you in determining your risk tolerance and growth needs, and suggest an allocation between various types of investments. It's important to have a working knowledge of the investments you are buying and the associated costs. If you can't explain your investment to a fifth grader, then you don't understand it well enough yourself. If you have been auto-enrolled into your company's 401(k) plan, be sure to meet with the advisor to select your funds. The auto-selected funds might not be the best options for you.

How should I choose my financial planner/investment advisor? Too many of us fall into the trap of selecting an advisor because we know and like them. This person is a friend, relative, or someone we know from church. It's not a bad idea to ask the financially healthy people in your life for recommendations, but be sure to do your own research. Find out how long they have been in the business and how they are getting paid to manage your investments.

Personally, I prefer independent advisors because they charge a flat percentage of your assets (typically 1% or less per year) for their fee rather than receiving commissions from mutual fund companies for selling you their investments. Interview two or three advisors, and ask to speak with one or two of their current clients before making your choice. You want an advisor who has the patience to explain investing in a way you can understand. If you feel confused, move on to someone else. If something feels off in your gut, please trust that feeling!

Should I save for retirement before I put money away for my kids' college? Yes! Please save for your own retirement *before* you save for your kids' college expenses! There are many ways to fund college: scholarships, grants, work-study programs, part-time jobs, and student loans. There's no such thing as a retirement loan for you! There's only one way to fund your retirement and that's you investing the money, early and often.

ACTION ITEMS

If you are not contributing to your retirement account, begin doing so right away.

Meet with your financial advisor at least once a year to review your investments and make sure you are on track for retirement.

If you're not happy with your current advisor, ask for recommendations and interview at least two people before making a change.

Read or listen to at least one book or podcast on investing for retirement.

Part Six

Your Bright Future

Chapter 38

TRUSTING AGAIN

I f you're fresh off your divorce, the last thing you want to think about is trusting someone again, especially in the area of money. You need time to heal, and it's usually not smart to jump into a new relationship without dealing with the issues of your past. However, there likely will come a time when you are ready for a new relationship, and it's important to learn to trust again.

Please don't wait until you're engaged or moving in together to start having money conversations with your new significant other. When you first start dating someone, just observe how he talks about and handles money. Does he allude to the fact that he has a ton of bills, credit card debt, or big student loan payments? Does he always insist on paying for dates, or insist on you paying? Or is he "even-steven" when it comes to going out? Does he admire financially successful individuals or refer to them as "greedy rich people"? These observations will give you clues as to how he thinks about and handles money.

When you begin to get more serious with your honey, that's the time to start having more in-depth conversations as money topics come up. One of the best financial conversation starters is this question: "How did your parents handle money when you were growing up?" And this follow-up: "Do you agree with their approach?" This will give you insight into your partner's money story and might uncover differences you need to discuss in depth.

Once you are officially engaged, I highly recommend you take a personal finance class together. Some churches have a financial component to their required premarital program. At the very least, read or listen to a book on money management together. I've had countless couples tell me that reading *Money Is Emotional* together spurred in-depth conversations that improved both their relationship and their finances. It might also be helpful to have a few sessions with a financial coach to help you navigate the combining of your finances. This is especially true if there are stepchildren involved or one of you is coming into the relationship with a disproportionate amount of either debt or assets.

This is also the time to get "financially naked" with your significant other. But please do not give anyone access to your credit cards or checking accounts until you are legally married. I made that mistake with Jeff, and I ended up being responsible for all the debt he helped me accumulate. You should both disclose all of your assets, debts, and credit history. The goal is not to shame or judge each other. When you "become one" in marriage, that means financially as well! You're improving your relationship with money, and you want to make sure that your partner is going to be on board.

"Financial transparency is incredibly important in a marriage. Typically, one spouse is in control of the finances. Educating and familiarizing oneself will go a long way for your relationship as a whole, and will give you more confidence and certainty," says divorce attorney Bryan Goldstein.

There should not be any hidden purchases, debt, or savings accounts going into marriage. Talk about how you are going to handle the day-to-day financial transactions in your house. Who is going to be responsible for making bill payments, buying groceries, purchasing items for the house? Is all of your money going to be in one joint account, or will you keep some spending money separate?

Remember, just because your significant other does something different from you with their money, it doesn't necessarily mean it's wrong. You might project your ex's mistakes onto your significant other. If your ex was controlling with money, you might see any attempt to have a discussion about your spending habits as an attack on your newfound financial freedom. If either of you experienced financial drama in your past relationship, I highly recommend working with a financial counselor to navigate those issues before you walk down the aisle.

If you have these conversations prior to getting married and work out the differences, you'll be much more likely to have a strong, loving marriage that lasts. However, you may discover there are deal breaker issues. Isn't it better you find this out now rather than *after* the wedding?

QUESTIONS TO CONSIDER & ACTION ITEMS:

What will be the hardest part of learning to trust someone again, especially regarding money?

What money behaviors in your ex do you strongly dislike?

If you are dating someone new, observe what they say about money and their behavior. Is there any evidence that you should or shouldn't trust them as far as finances are concerned?

Chapter 39

HIS MONEY, HER MONEY, AND OUR MONEY

If and when you get remarried, how should you handle your money together as a couple? First, let me say that deliberately hiding money or debt from your spouse is a horrible idea. *Separate money does not mean secret money!* If you had any past drama or trauma around money, you might be inclined to just keep everything separate. If you don't have any joint accounts, you're living as "financial roommates." This means you might miss out on opportunities to communicate on a deeper level about what's important to you. If both you and your husband are comfortable combining all of your finances into joint accounts, then by all means, go for it. Make sure both of your names are on all accounts so you both have access.

I find that many couples who enter into a second (or third) marriage prefer a hybrid approach. This usually involves opening a joint account to which you both contribute for your household expenses. If your incomes are not similar, I recommend splitting the expenses proportionally. For example, if you make 40% of your household income, you contribute an amount equal to 40% of the household expenses. The downfall to this approach is that it can get complicated, and might involve more work and communication than your finances being completely separate or combined. Thankfully, there are personal finance tools like AskZeta.com that allow you to create and track hybrid spending plans.

The reason a couple might want to separate some of their money is to reduce (not increase) disagreements over spending. Having separate accounts for your discretionary spending money can foster a sense of responsibility and freedom. Having fun money in your own account means you have the control to spend the money as you please *without* owing an explanation to your husband. Just be sure to decide as a couple in advance how much money will go to each spouse's discretionary spending account every month.

This idea works beautifully for my husband and me. We have three checking accounts: our household bill account, my checking account, and his checking account. The bank automatically transfers money from our personal checking accounts to the household bill account every two weeks. We pay the utilities, insurance, groceries, and general household expenses from this account. From our separate checking accounts, we each pay for our own gas, entertainment, clothing, and other fun stuff. This way, Nick doesn't complain that I'm spending "too much" on manicures, wine, or clothes. And I don't complain when he spends his fun money on the latest electronics or a rare coin for his collection.

When you're part of a blended family, having some money in separate accounts can be very beneficial. A great deal of turmoil and disagreements can erupt between spouses when stepchildren (and even grandchildren) are in the picture. Not only do parenting styles differ, but also spending choices. It helps for husbands and wives to agree on a total amount to spend on "her kids" and "his kids," and then for each parent to decide individually how to allocate the total among their own kids and the various categories. If you've already agreed to the total amount and are sticking to it, there's no reason to bicker over the details! I know some women who keep their child support money in a separate account for this purpose. If you're thinking of remarrying and either of you have children, it's vitally important to consult an attorney for the proper estate planning as well.

My preference is for my married clients to keep the majority of their money in joint accounts. If you're married and are still keeping all of your money separate, it might be a sign of trust issues that should be talked over with a counselor or therapist. Deliberately hiding credit cards or even savings accounts from your spouse is a terrible idea. I also firmly believe spouses should have access to all accounts. Remember, the reason a couple may want to separate some of their money is to *reduce* disagreements over spending.

Here's an important FYI, and a potential exception to my preference for joint accounts. If you receive an inheritance, keep it in a separate account in your name only, with your spouse as the beneficiary. Transfer amounts as you need or want to spend it into your joint account, rather than all of it. If this marriage doesn't work out, inherited funds kept separate are not usually considered marital assets. This means you keep 100% of your inherited money in that separate account in the event of divorce.

Please note if you and your spouse decide to keep any separate accounts, be sure to list the other as the account beneficiary. If one of you dies without a beneficiary listed, you'll have to go through the probate court system to get access to the money that's rightfully yours. This can easily take 60 to 90 days or longer. And if you need the money to live on and pay bills, that could be a major problem on top of your grief.

The one major drawback of not having your spouse's name on your account is lack of access in the case of a medical emergency.

If you're in a car accident, lying in the hospital unconscious, your spouse won't be able to access any money in separate accounts to pay bills on your behalf. You might still decide to keep some of your accounts completely separate, and that's absolutely okay! I simply want you to be aware of the pros and cons of doing so. Even though my husband and I have some of our money separate, almost all accounts have both of our names on them.

If you're not married yet, you should keep your accounts separate until you are legally married. Engagements are occasionally canceled and it can be an enormous pain to have your ex-boyfriend/fiancé removed from your accounts.

QUESTIONS TO CONSIDER:

How was the money handled in your previous relationship (together, separate, or a combination)?

What did you like and dislike about the money being handled that way and why?

How would you like the finances to be handled if and when you enter into a new relationship?

Chapter 40

KIDS & MONEY

I t's unavoidable; you're going to make some hard financial choices that directly affect your children because of your divorce. This could involve moving to a smaller house in a different neighborhood. It might mean taking your kids out of private school or scaling back on extra-curricular activities because it's straining your finances. I know it's hard to watch your kids suffer the consequences of divorce, especially where the money is concerned.

Please hear this: Your primary responsibility to your children is to provide a loving and financially stable situation for them during this transition. Yes, the mom guilt is real, but please don't risk bankruptcy trying to insulate your kids from the financial consequences of your divorce. Some women consciously or unconsciously try to "make up" for the divorce by buying their kids more stuff. It's important to remember that your children want your *presence* more than they want your *presents*.

"Help your child understand your financial situation and the changes that are coming by sharing specific examples of what to expect. Tell them the truth but maintain a healthy boundary in the wording, keeping in mind their emotional age. Create a safe space for your child (and you) to feel the feelings that come up and allow them to be a part of the decision-making process around changes that affect them. Involve middle-school and high-school aged children in problem-solving some of the solutions. You might be surprised by how capable and creative they are!"" says Maria Natapov, Stepparenting Coach.

It's easy to fall into the trap of trying to one-up your ex financially with your kids, especially when the holidays roll around. You can't control what your ex does with money, but you can have positive and productive financial conversations with your kids.

Moms often ask me, "What's the best way to teach my kids about money?" The first step is getting and staying financially healthy yourself. Your kids are watching you and listening to you. The things you do and say about money are going to leave more of an impression than any financial guru's book or board game. And now that you know the importance of your money mindset, you want to ensure you don't pass on faulty money beliefs and narratives to your children.

You don't need a formal money curriculum to introduce your children to money management. Often the most profound lessons we can teach our kids about saving, spending, and giving are interwoven into everyday life. Lead by example!

How early should you start teaching your kids about money? You can begin the basics with kids as young as four years old, when they're learning to count coins and paper money. This is a good age to make the connection between work and money. Pay them to do some (not all) of their chores. Let them save up their money, and take them to the store to buy a toy. It's best to keep it simple at this age. However, you might be surprised by how much young children are capable of absorbing.

If you want to stick with cash, grade school age kids can graduate to a system of three piggy banks or envelopes, one each for giving, saving, and spending. Or you can use a product like Greenlight, which is a debit card you load with money as your child earns it. Greenlight allows you to control the places they spend the money and even put monthly category limits in place. If you haven't already, take your child to the bank with you to open a savings account. There are plenty of opportunities to teach kids about prices, coupons, and sales tax during your weekly trips to the grocery store.

Kids who are in middle school might be earning some money outside of chores by babysitting their siblings, having a lemonade stand, or walking the neighbors' dogs. This is a good time to give them more autonomy in their spending, especially if they have proven themselves to be good little money managers.

By the time your kids get to high school, it's time for their first checking account. Deposit the money you'd normally spend on them for clothing, sports, and entertainment, and teach them to manage it themselves. They will spend their money differently this way than if you are just paying for everything. It will reinforce that there's a limit to money, and choices need to be made. Teach them how to balance their account when the monthly statement is available. Your high schooler will likely need "training wheels" the first few months of having a checking account, so stay involved until they get the hang of it. This is the time to discuss things like car payments and insurance, student loans, and credit cards.

"Should I get my teen a credit card?" It's something parents ask me on a regular basis. I'd advise opening a low-limit secured credit card, which will allow your teen to start building their credit history. With a secured credit card, your teen is depositing the same amount of money as the credit card limit into a savings account held by the bank as security. If they get in trouble and can't pay the credit card, the bank takes the money from the savings account to pay it off. It's best to teach them how to responsibly use a credit card by paying it in full monthly while they are under your watchful guidance.

The bottom line is this: You need to train your children and give them good resources for wise money management. By weaving personal finance lessons into everyday life situations, you will set your kids up for money success in adulthood — which is a big parenting win!

QUESTIONS TO CONSIDER & ACTION ITEMS:

How are the financial consequences of your divorce affecting your kids? How does this make you feel?

In what ways are you tempted to do potentially unhealthy things in your finances to insulate your kids from the consequences of divorce?

Decide on some age-appropriate ways to talk to your kids about money, using real-world examples.

Chapter 41

GRATITUDE

*A*re you grateful for all of the things you currently have? You should be, because you are rich! *Don't believe me?* If you live anywhere in North America, you are fortunate enough to be in the top 10% of the world's wealth. You might not feel like you're rich if you're not driving a BMW or a Mercedes Benz. You don't belong to a country club or own a yacht. Yet, you are still rich.

Do you have clean drinking water? Are you able to take a hot shower whenever you want? Do you have food in your pantry and refrigerator? Do you own a car? Do you own a house? Do you sleep on a mattress? Do you make more than $2.00 per day?

If you answered yes to most or all of these questions, you're indeed richer than 90% of the world. It's easy to forget how good we really have it. You see celebrities' social media feeds and think your life would somehow be better if you had an indoor swimming pool, a Maserati, and a six-car garage. It's easy to forget to be grateful for the many blessings already in your possession. There's nothing wrong with wanting to do better financially, but *if you fail to practice gratitude on a regular basis, you'll never be happy with what you have, no matter how much it is.*

Let's say you have two friends, Joella and Emma. Joella never expresses gratitude to you for anything. She never says thank you when you treat her to lunch, send her flowers to cheer her up, or watch her kids. Emma, on the other hand, thanks you every single time you do something nice for her. She posts pics and thanks you publicly on social media for birthday gifts. She appreciates and reciprocates when you offer moral support or practical help. Which friend is going to attract more blessings in her life from you? Although you love both of your friends, you're probably going to bless Emma more because of her attitude of gratitude. God/the Universe responds the same way to our gratitude!

Every day, I write down three things I'm grateful for on a legal pad. My entries include thankfulness for time spent with friends and family, financial blessings, delicious food, the beauty of nature, and simply the ability to wake up and get out of bed in the morning. If you prefer a pretty journal to do this, permission is granted to buy one! It doesn't matter so much how or where you write your gratitude items; just do it. By the end of the year, you'll have a list of almost 1,100 things you're thankful for! If I'm in a down mood, it helps me to revisit my gratitude list and remember the many reasons I have to be happy and thankful.

Does it mean you're not grateful if you want more and better things for yourself and your family? Absolutely not! I currently have a picture of a house with a gorgeous swimming pool on my financial vision board. Yes, of course, I want it! But in the meantime, I am grateful for my current home, and I take excellent care of it. Are you grateful for the things you already have? Do you take good care of them while you're hoping and believing for something even better? Being grateful for what we already have creates a sense of peace and satisfaction deep inside of us. It's okay to desire more; just ensure that you're also grateful for what you already have.

Here are some easy ways to cultivate gratitude on a regular basis:

- **Every day, write down three things you're grateful for.** I keep a legal pad on my kitchen table and do this first thing in the morning while I enjoy my coffee. It takes less than three minutes to do! If a feeling of lack creeps in, all I have to do is flip through the legal pad to remind myself of the awesome things, experiences, and people I have in my life. If you do this every day, you'll have intentionally expressed gratitude 1,100 times in one year!

- **Every time you receive or find money, say "thank you!"** Whenever I get an email notification from PayPal or Stripe that someone joined my membership, purchased a course, or bought a book from me, I say thank you. Yes, out loud! If I receive a rebate check or a refund, I say thank you. If I find a quarter on the ground, I pick it up and say thank you. If we don't practice gratitude in the little things, we can forget to do it with the big things.

- **Every time you pay a bill, say, "Thank you for the money!"** I know, this one sounds weird, but I got this idea from the book *The Magic* by Rhonda Byrne (author of *The Secret*). It's about developing a positive money consciousness and creating an attitude of abundance and gratitude. As I'm paying my bills, I write on the bill itself, "Thank you for the money." In doing this, I'm thanking God/the Universe for blessing me with the money to pay my bills. It is a reminder to be grateful for the financial resources you already have at your disposal.

- **Express gratitude in advance!** I already mentioned this in the chapter about money mantras. You can use the phrases "I'm so happy and grateful…" or "I'm so joyful and thankful…" and attach your money goals to them. For example "I'm so happy and grateful I'm living in my dream home on 25 acres with a saltwater swimming pool, paid for with cash!" I'm demonstrating to God (the Universe) that I'm grateful for the things I want even before they're delivered to me in the real world.

ACTION ITEMS:

Make a daily practice of writing down at least three things you're grateful for each day.

Select one other gratitude practice from this chapter, and begin doing it immediately.

Chapter 42

GENEROSITY

Generosity is an important part of a healthy Prosperity Plan. Being generous with charitable causes, religious organizations, and other people goes hand-in-hand with gratitude. Generosity is a natural response when you're thankful, because you recognize how blessed you truly are. The amount you give to charity is a very personal decision, and I recommend you make it a part of your monthly spending plan. Personally, I donate 10% of all my income. If your financial situation is strained, you might need to start with a smaller percentage, and that's okay!

I began my generosity practice when I hit rock bottom. I remember my dad explaining the benefits of giving and generosity to me a week after I left my ex. "How can I afford to give anything away? I'm homeless!" I wailed. "Honey," he patiently replied, "You're living in the spare bedroom of my house in a golf course community. You're not homeless. I'm happy to drive you downtown so you can see those people who actually are homeless." Yes, I was being dramatic and feeling sorry for myself!

My Dad encouraged me to start donating a small amount every month to a charity. I picked the local homeless shelter and began donating $40 a month. Every time I wrote the check, it reminded me that, although my current situation wasn't ideal, I still had so much to be grateful for. I had a warm and safe house to stay in, a soft bed, food on the table, a good job, and a family who loved me.

Twenty-two years later, I still donate every month to the same local homeless shelter. It's amazing to think of the positive impact my donations have had on countless people over the years. Generosity is good for us – not just emotionally, but also physically.

According to the Cleveland Clinic, the following health benefits are associated with giving: lower blood pressure, increased self-esteem, less depression, lower stress levels, longer life, and greater happiness. In a 2006 study, the National Institutes of Health studied the MRIs of people who gave to various charities. They found that giving stimulates the reward center in the brain, releasing endorphins and creating what is known as the "helper's high." If everyone was addicted to this "helper's high," imagine how the world would change for the better!

ACTION ITEMS:

Decide on at least one charity or religious organization to donate to each and every month.

Decide on the amount and put it into your monthly spending plan.

Chapter 43

OVER-GIVING

Generosity is a wonderful thing, but if you don't have healthy boundaries in place, it can get out of balance. How do you ensure your generosity doesn't cross the line into over-giving? You must learn to say no nicely, yet firmly.

Let's be honest. Having to say no to money requests tops the list of awkward conversations. A friend or family member asks to borrow money or wants you to co-sign a loan for them. You don't have the money – or you just plain don't want to. You know lending money can change the dynamic of the relationship and lead to resentment if the money's not paid back as agreed. Thankfully, there's a way to make these tough talks easier!

Make it a personal policy. The easiest way to avoid awkward money requests is to shut them down immediately with a personal "no-lending policy." Yes, it's that simple! Make it a policy to NEVER loan people money or cosign loans. When someone requests help, just say "I have a personal policy to never lend money to friends or family." If they ask why, you can say, "My relationships are too important to have money come between us." (I mean, how can they argue with that?) This policy closes the door on further conversation, because you don't loan money to anyone, no matter the situation or who it is.

Don't drag it out. When someone makes a money request of you, it's totally acceptable to respond with "I need to think about it" or "I want to sleep on it." Sometimes it's easier to weigh the pros and cons of giving or lending money without the person right in front of you, staring at you with those sad puppy dog eyes.

If you decide to sleep on it, don't drag it out for more than a day or two. Otherwise, you're going to agonize over the decision and the other person will likely be anxious, too. If you're going to say no, it's best to get it over with quickly, like pulling off a bandage.

Be clear, be concise, be nice. Confusion multiplies when you multiply your words. Don't talk in circles or try to soften up your "no." Doing so will only encourage the person to try and persuade you to change your mind. Use the word "won't" instead of "can't." "Can't" implies that you *want* to give or lend them the money, but there's some obstacle in your way. It invites the other person to brainstorm ways you can help them. "Won't" states that you will not be lending them the money. Period. End of discussion.

Here are some ways to phrase "no" clearly, concisely, and, of course, nicely:

- "I won't be able to give (or lend) at this time."
- "It's not feasible in my finances to help."
- "I'm not comfortable co-signing for you."

Notice that none of these examples explains WHY. There's a reason for that! It's unnecessary. You don't owe the other person an explanation, only a yes or no answer. If they press you, look them in the eye and say, "No is the final answer."

Offer to help in other ways. Maybe you don't want to co-sign for your sister's new car, but you're willing to carpool to work with her, since your companies are two miles apart. You don't want to lend your grown son cash, but you're happy to buy him some food while you're at the grocery store.

You're still helping to alleviate their need without money directly in the equation. They'll either graciously accept your alternative help, or they'll find another way to come up with the money. This is especially effective for people who are financially manipulative or irresponsible.

Create an "Abundance Fund." I'm all for you being a generous person. I want you to include giving in your Prosperity Plan! I love the concept of the Abundance Fund, which author and cofounder of Wealthquest, James Lenhoff, discusses in his book *Living a Rich Life*. Essentially, once you've created your spending plan, including the extras and fun stuff, you put the excess cash into a dedicated account for the sole purpose of giving it away.

The next time someone asks you for financial help, you just check your Abundance Fund account, and decide if you want to give (not lend) the person the money they need. If they do happen to pay you back, the funds go back into the Abundance Fund to bless the next person. Because sometimes you really want to say YES to someone's money request. The Abundance Fund ensures you're doing it in such a way that you won't damage your own financial wellbeing.

QUESTIONS TO CONSIDER:

Is there someone in your life who asks you for money on a regular basis?

Do you feel like you're being taken advantage of or resentful when you help?

Do you need to institute a "no lending to friends or family" policy?

Chapter 44

FINANCIAL ENABLING

hat if you're already embroiled in an unhealthy pattern of over-giving, to the point of financially enabling someone? I used to be a big-time financial enabler. I was young and in love, and I thought with enough emotional and financial support, I could help Jeff become all that I thought he could be. Over the course of the seven-year relationship, I cleaned up countless financial messes for him. Unfortunately, the more I "helped" Jeff, the worse things became.

You see, my help wasn't really helping him personally or financially. I shielded Jeff from the negative consequences of his financial misbehavior, so he never learned his lesson. I became bitter and resentful over always having to clean up his messes. *But it wasn't his fault; it was mine.*

What's the difference between helping and enabling? Helping is doing something for someone that they are unable to do for themselves. Enabling is doing something for someone that they can and should be doing for themselves.

I frequently see this situation come up during my coaching sessions with parents. Many times, they are "helping" their irresponsible adult children and constantly bailing them out of their financial disasters. It's definitely a sensitive subject that can cause lots of drama and conflict.

Here are the signs of financial enabling:

- The person expects you to help and uses guilt to try to manipulate you.
- The person makes the same kinds of financial mistakes over and over.
- The person seems to get worse, not better, after you help them.
- You are suffering financially as a result of helping the other person.
- The situation is a constant source of stress — and you feel bitter and resentful.

So how do you break the cycle of financial enabling? The first and hardest step to breaking this cycle is admitting that you are a financial enabler and you are part of the problem. You're shielding your loved one from the financial consequences of their behavior, which isn't a good thing for either of you.

Once you have reached this conclusion, you need to arrange a sit-down meeting to discuss the situation. Be prepared for the other person to be upset and even to say that you are unloving or uncaring for letting them face their own consequences. (I have to add here that counseling might also be needed to work out these issues in a family or relationship. I also highly recommend reading the classic book *Boundaries* by Dr. Henry Cloud.)

Depending on the situation, you might need to set up a reasonable timeline for change. For example, let's say your 28-year-old able-bodied son or daughter is still living at home, not paying any rent or otherwise contributing to the household expenses. During your discussion, set a timeline that they must either move out or begin paying $X in rent to you within 60 or 90 days. The difficult part for you will be sticking to your timeline *no matter what*. It's likely that the person will test you to see if you are serious, so be expecting it.

Now, please understand that I'm not saying that you should never help your loved ones when they are having a hard time. The above guidelines are for the repeat offender who is always in financial trouble and seems to get worse — not better — when you "help" them. If you have a friend or relative who's normally a very responsible person who comes to you because of an unforeseen situation, such as a job loss or divorce, by all means help them!

But only assist them if you can afford to GIVE them the money (not lend it). If they happen to pay you back later when they get back on their feet, great. If not, don't be offended by it. *If you think you'll be mad if they never pay you back the money, then don't give it to them.* Period. Many relationships have been ruined because of this very situation.

QUESTIONS TO CONSIDER & ACTION ITEMS:

Are you caught in a pattern of financially enabling someone to your own detriment?

If so, use the steps outlined in this chapter to break the cycle and set healthy boundaries.

Chapter 45

BE YOUR OWN BEST FRIEND

he year was 1998. My best friend, Nicholle, came to me with a dilemma. Here's what she said, "Christine, my boyfriend, Ben, is in jail because of a DUI. He called me collect and said he's going to go crazy if I don't post bail for him and get him out of there. The problem is that I'm living paycheck to paycheck and don't have the money to do it. The only possible way I can bail him out is if I cash in the stock certificates my dad bought me for my 21st birthday. Do you think I should do it? Ben's really pressuring me."

My response went something like this, "Are you crazy? Of course not! Don't you dare cash in those stocks your dad bought you for your birthday! Ben's in jail because he chose to be stupid and drive drunk. He's lucky he didn't kill somebody! Ben's getting what he deserves; let him rot in jail for all I care."

I couldn't believe Nicholle was considering it! Why would she take the financial consequences of Ben's behaviors?

Unfortunately, she didn't listen to me. She drove to the financial planner's office and requested the stock be liquidated for cash.

I have a confession to make. The above story isn't exactly true. It wasn't Nicholle's boyfriend who was in jail; it was mine.

At a posh restaurant overlooking the skyline of Cincinnati in December 1994, my Dad presented me with 21 shares of stock in Fifth Third Bank, the company I worked for at the time. It was a very cool and thoughtful 21st birthday gift. I remember thinking it would be a great seed to my financial nest egg that would surely flourish as time passed.

Fast forward three and half years later. Jeff didn't come home after a night of partying, driving my car. I received a collect call from the county jail to find out he'd received a DUI and my car was impounded. Because of Jeff's spotty work habits, I had no money in the bank and would have to pay some bills late in order to get my car back. I definitely had no money to post his bail. Jeff insisted I "do whatever it takes" to get him out of there. The only assets I had were those stock certificates my dad had given me for my birthday. My only choice was to cash those in so I could post Jeff's bail, right? People are more important than money, I reasoned. If it were me, I'd want him to do the same for me.

However, it wouldn't be me in jail! As a teenager, I never even snuck out of my house for fear my parents would be disappointed in me if they ever found out. I'm a responsible person down deep into my core. But I reasoned with myself that bailing Jeff out was the right thing to do. *Why?* Because I allowed myself to be emotionally manipulated. Maybe it's happened to you, too.

Is there a way to pull the plug on these erratic emotions when it comes to making decisions about our money? Yes! I call it the "Be Your Own Best Friend" technique. In the two opening paragraphs of this chapter, I restated my dilemma as if it were happening to my best friend, Nicholle. If you go back and look at my response, there's nothing wishy-washy about it. My reaction is swift and visceral. There is no way Nicholle should pay for Ben's mistakes.

If you are grappling with a money situation that's emotionally charged, write out the facts of the situation as if it's happening to your best friend. Write out names and details. Then write down what advice you would give your friend. *Guess what?* Each of us should be our own very best friend. Then be smart enough to take your own advice.

It can be hard for us to recognize when the people we love are violating our healthy money boundaries. Growing up we hear things like "The love of money is the root of evil" and "People are more important than money." Be aware that people may use statements like these to guilt us into doing what they want. You're not selfish for setting and enforcing healthy money boundaries in your life. **You are not responsible for the financial consequences of other people's actions.**

You can also use the "Be Your Own Best Friend" technique for less dramatic money decisions. What if you're considering purchasing a newer vehicle and you're not sure if it's the right move? Simply write out the pros and cons of the situation as if your best friend is pondering the same decision. What questions might you ask of your best friend in this situation? "How many miles are on your current car? Does it need major repairs? How much do you owe on your current car? Do you have cash saved up for the new one you're looking to buy?" It's easier to frame purchase decisions this way because it dials down the emotional intensity. If you see the red convertible you've always wanted at the car dealership, your heart can hijack your wallet before you even know what happened! Back away from the convertible, take a deep breath, and find someplace quiet where you can objectively evaluate the money decision you're about to make.

Often, we know deep down what we *should* do, but our heightened emotions hijack our common sense. Another way to be your own best friend as you are dealing with the fallout of divorce is to take good care of yourself emotionally, physically, and financially.

Revisit your spending plan, and ensure you've earmarked some money every month to pamper yourself in a healthy way. Don't neglect self-care during this time! Be your own best friend.

QUESTIONS TO CONSIDER & ACTION ITEMS:

In what ways have you ignored your intuition about money and later suffered the consequences?

What emotionally charged decision are you wrestling with right now?

Write out this situation as if it's happening to your best friend, not you.

What advice would you give her?

What will you do this week or this month to nurture yourself? How much money do you have earmarked for taking care of yourself?

Chapter 46

FORGIVENESS

*A*re you holding onto resentment or anger over a past money situation with your ex? Maybe he secretly racked up tens of thousands of dollars in credit card debt, spending money on his new girlfriend. Maybe he hid cash from you in an attempt to pay you less money in the divorce settlement. Maybe your ex had a drug or drinking problem and ran your personal finances into the ground. Maybe you're still beating *yourself* up over past money mistakes you made, as I used to.

While writing my first book, *Money Is Emotional: Prevent Your Heart from Hijacking Your Wallet,* I found myself becoming very emotional as I wrote out my money stories on the page. (Go figure, right?) I felt surprised by my strong reactions as I remembered the details of the situations from my past. At first, I thought I might be harboring some resentment toward Jeff, and maybe I hadn't completely forgiven him. Later, it hit me like a ton of bricks. *The person I most needed to forgive was me.* I cringed internally when I retold certain stories about my past, still feeling regret over them, almost two decades later.

I decided to write a letter to my younger self, forgiving her once and for all for the mistakes, both financial and relational, she made during that seven-year period. I found several pictures of myself from that time, and I imagined I was talking to "younger me" as I wrote the letter. Below is an excerpt from it.

Dear Christine,

The reason I'm writing this letter is to let you know once and for all, I forgive you. I forgive you for all the stupid decisions you made with money because of emotion. I know you were trying to put love before money, and you didn't understand healthy boundaries and the importance of caring for and respecting yourself, which includes your finances.

I know you loved Jeff and you wanted to help him. You saw the potential in Jeff, the best version of himself he could be, if only he really wanted it. As time went on, your relationship became more lopsided and increasingly codependent. You began to go against what you knew was right deep down inside to keep the peace. You always hated conflict and eventually caved into Jeff's wishes so the fighting would stop. Every time you did that, you dimmed your light just a little bit more.

I forgive you for selling your Fifth Third Bank stock, a gift from Dad, to come up with Jeff's bail money. Although Dad has never said it, I feel like this really hurt his feelings by taking his gift and essentially throwing it away. This is the money mistake — although not the biggest one dollar-wise — that was the most regrettable. It certainly wasn't the only emotional money mistake you made.

Some of the other memorable ones include: purposely bouncing checks to buy groceries, numerous visits to payday lenders, allowing Jeff to drive my car and the resulting repair bills, credit cards and consolidation loans taken out, and pawning my grandmother's rings to bail Jeff's friend out of jail. Thankfully those rings were recovered. For all of those things and more, I forgive you.

I forgive you for not knowing when to say "no" and stand up for yourself. The great news is this is no longer a problem for you! And none of these past experiences are wasted. You're now teaching and coaching other people to become financially healthy and to make wise decisions in the midst of emotional money situations. God has not wasted your pain. He has turned it into something beautiful to help others heal from their financial wounds. God has also brought you into this relationship with your wonderful husband, Nick. He is a good man, providing for you financially and emotionally. Nick loves and appreciates your love and your light, and never tries to quench it.

I forgive you for not leaving Jeff sooner. Although it caused more pain in the short term, it all worked out in the long run. If you had left sooner, you might not have met and started dating Nick. You also might not have some of the stories — painful as they are — that really connect with your coaching clients.

Once and for all, I forgive you, Christine. Without your experiences, I wouldn't be the confident, brave Financial Dignity® Coach and author who I am today. I love you, and I wouldn't change a thing.

Love,
Your Older "Sister," Christine

Do you need to write a letter like this to yourself or to someone else who caused you pain around a money issue? I strongly encourage you to do so. After I wrote this letter to my younger self, I felt like a huge weight of guilt and shame had been lifted off my shoulders.

"Give yourself grace while transitioning through divorce," says Melissa Joy, CFP®, CDFA®. "Practice self-care and speak as kindly to yourself as you would your best friend."

If you're writing a letter to someone else who hurt you, *don't send it to them.* This letter is for you, not for them. This emotional baggage has been weighing you down on your journey to financial health. Write the letter, read it out loud, and then safely burn it or shred it. You don't need that heavy burden anymore. Let it go.

ACTION ITEMS:

Write a letter of forgiveness. DO NOT SEND IT! This is for you, not them.

Read it out loud, and then safely burn or shred it.

Chapter 47

RAISE YOUR FINANCIAL IQ

"As I was going through my divorce, I had to research and understand things in the financial world that I was never familiarized with before," divorced woman and author Allison K. Dagney says. "I was fearful my ex would take advantage of my lack of knowledge since he was the money expert and I had no knowledge of financial matters. I took initiative to learn so he couldn't steal what was rightfully mine."

After I left Jeff, it took me several years to get financially healthy and feel peaceful about my money. I mastered my spending, built up my savings, and paid off all of my debt. As my wealth started to grow, there were new things I needed to learn and master to continue feeling peaceful and confident about my money.

I dove into learning about investing, insurance, tax planning, and more advanced money mindset work. I am still learning about these financial topics, not just for my own benefit, but also for yours! When it comes to money mindset and management, you never stop learning and growing. As your financial assets increase and your goals evolve, there will be new things you need to learn and do. Just like your physical health, you've never "arrived" at perfect financial health.

Are you invested in raising your money IQ? Which area of personal finance do you need to focus on first? Here's my recommended order: money mindset, managing spending, debt reduction, saving, retirement and investing, and finally, estate planning, taxes, and insurance.

How many books have you read (or listened to) this past year? The two excuses I hear from women as to why they don't read much are: 1) they struggle with reading, or 2) they don't have time. Fortunately, you don't need a physical book to raise your money IQ! Download an audiobook or queue up a podcast on your phone and listen while sitting in traffic, during your workout, or while getting ready in the morning. It's certainly better for your brain and your mood than listening to the news or talk radio. There are a multitude of ways you can increase your money IQ based on your needs and preferences, including books, videos, podcasts, audiobooks, online courses and memberships, and one-on-one coaching. I've included a Recommended Resources section at the end of this book to get you started!

Do you want to do better financially this year than you did last year? I do! Well, if you want to earn more, you need to learn more. As the late, great Jim Rohn said, "Formal education will make you a living; self-education will make you a fortune!" The good news is that self-education is available to anyone with a library card, laptop, or cell phone.

If you want your financial situation to grow and evolve, you have to grow and evolve. Achieving Financial Dignity® after a divorce or breakup is a journey. If you feel yourself backsliding a bit, go back and revisit the chapters in this book that address the emotional or financial struggles you're currently facing.

Be sure to invest in your self-improvement and earmark money in your spending plan to expand your knowledge and your income! What you focus on expands. Paying attention to your money pays positive dividends!

Don't forget: You're in a relationship with money. Respect it. Spend quality time with it. Love it! If you do, money will support your goals and dreams. Yes, it is possible for you and money to live happily ever after!

QUESTIONS TO CONSIDER & ACTION ITEMS:

Which area of personal finance do you need to invest some time (and money) into learning more?

What resources are you going to use to raise your money IQ?

Schedule financial education time on your calendar!

$\mathcal{C}hapter$ 48

Moving Confidently into the Future

The future is a blank slate, which can be exciting, scary, or a little of both. The thoughts you think and the actions you take today will shape your financial future. Don't make the mistake of thinking that divorce or a traumatic breakup is the end of the world. Yes, it might be the end of life as you've known it up until this point, but that's not necessarily a bad thing.

For three months after I left Jeff, I lived in my Dad's spare bedroom with a negative net worth, a dismal credit score, and a poor self-image. Those things didn't change overnight with a snap of a finger. They improved a little bit at a time, day by day. It took me a year to pay off all the credit card debt from that relationship. It took another two years to pay off my car. It took almost five years before my credit score returned to a healthy range. But I never gave up. I was (and still am) committed to improving my relationship with money.

I focused on what I wanted out of life, and how money could support my happiness. I found friends and mentors who were positive influences on me, financially and otherwise. I started dating my husband Nick, who walked the talk when it came to wise money decisions. Let me tell you, there is nothing sexier than a financially responsible man when you've been previously engaged to a freeloader! *"You max out your retirement accounts? That is sooo hot!"*

I left Jeff over twenty years ago. When I think about that time in my life, it feels like it happened to a different person. Nick and I have a wonderful, loving marriage. We frequently talk about our financial goals and dreams for the future. We have a high net worth, zero debt, and plenty of money in savings and investments.

When I left Jeff, the future was a blank slate, and I chose what the next chapters would say. And you can do the same for your own life. You have a bright future ahead, even if you can't see it around the bend yet. You just need to put one foot in front of the other each day, walking a little closer to the light.

I believe in you! You and money are going to do great things together.

Enjoy this Book?

YOU CAN MAKE A BIG DIFFERENCE!

I am so grateful for my committed and loyal readers! Your reviews are one of the best thank-yous I can receive.

Reviews are the most powerful tool I have as an author when it comes to bringing my books to the attention of other readers.

If you enjoyed this book, I would be very grateful if you could spend just five minutes leaving a review (it can be as short as you like) on the book's Amazon page.

Also by

CHRISTINE LUKEN

Money is Emotional:
Prevent Your Heart from Hijacking Your Wallet

If money is emotional, then why do we persist in trying to manage our personal finances logically? We already know what it takes to become financially healthy: Spend less than we make, pay down our debt, and save more money. Money management books, tools, and techniques abound, yet most of us don't utilize them. Maybe you've adopted the practice of ignoring money problems until they are barreling down on you like a tidal wave, as I once did. I know what it feels like to be drowning financially.

I'd like to propose a better alternative, one that doesn't require you to eat beans and rice or to spend hours updating budget spreadsheets. My approach to personal finance is called "Mindful Money Management." It is unique in that it harnesses the power of your emotions, so they can propel you forward like a rocket booster toward your Preferred Financial Destination. Yes, money is emotional, but you can prevent your heart from hijacking your wallet. Let me show you how. Available from Amazon and Audible.

Download the first three chapters at
www.MoneyIsEmotional.com

Manage Money Like a Boss:
A Financial Guide for Creative Entrepreneurs

You're doing what you love for a living, making a business out of your creativity, whether it's photography, fashion, music, marketing, writing, or crafting the perfect microbrew.

The only problem? Managing your business finances is a serious drag. Accounting is confusing. Taxes are scary. And most financial experts you know are intimidating. (Are they speaking another language?)

You deserve financial guidance that's simple to understand and implement, from someone who honors and appreciates your creativity. As both a writer and an accountant, I love both words and numbers. I will demystify money for you so it can become your best employee, rather than your worst nightmare.

This isn't just a book about business finance. We dive deep into some surprising things that impact your bottom line, to help you make more money, get more customers, and look like a pro. I will give you both the confidence and competence to manage your money like a BOSS. Available from Amazon.

Download the first three chapters at
www.ManageMoneyLikeABoss.com

Recommended Resources

I hope you will view this book as the beginning of your financial education, not the end. Here are books and other resources I recommend.

PERSONAL FINANCE:
- Financial Dignity® on Demand Membership
- *Money Is Emotional: Prevent Your Heart from Hijacking Your Wallet*, by Christine Luken
- *Retire Inspired: It's Not an Age; It's a Financial Number*, by Chris Hogan
- *Unshakeable: Your Financial Freedom Playbook*, by Tony Robbins
- *Living a Rich Life: The No-Regrets Guide to Building & Spending Wealth*, by James Lenhoff
- *The Sudden Wealth Solution: 12 Principles to Transform Sudden Wealth into Lasting Wealth*, by Robert Pagliarini
- *Women with Money: The Judgment-Free Guide to Creating the Joyful, Less Stressed, Purposeful (and Yes, Rich) Life You Deserve*, by Jean Chatzky
- *Smart Money, Smart Kids: Raising the Next Generation to Win with Money*, by Dave Ramsey and Rachel Cruze

MONEY MINDSET:

- The Magnetic Money Mindset™ Bundle
- *Secrets of the Millionaire Mind*, by T. Harv Eker
- *You Are a Badass at Making Money*, by Jen Sincero
- *The Science of Getting Rich: Your Master Key to Success*, by Wallace D. Wattles
- *Worthy: Boost Your Self-Worth to Grow Your Net Worth*, by Nancy Levin
- *Boundaries: When to Say Yes, How to Say No to Take Control of Your Life*, by Dr. Henry Cloud and Dr. John Townsend
- *Thank & Grow Rich: A 30-Day Experiment in Shameless Gratitude and Unabashed Joy*, by Pam Grout
- *The Miracle Equation: The Two Decisions That Move Your Biggest Goals from Possible, to Probable, to Inevitable*, by Hal Elrod

BUSINESS & ENTREPRENEURSHIP:

- *Manage Money Like a BOSS: A Financial Guide for Creative Entrepreneurs*, by Christine Luken
- *Your First Six Figures: Eight Keys to Unlocking Freedom, Flow, and Financial Success with Your Online Business*, by Jenn Scalia
- *Quitter: Closing the Gap Between Your Day Job & Your Dream Job*, by Jon Acuff
- *Profit First*, by Mike Michalowicz
- *The Time-Wealthy Investor 2.0: Your Real Estate Roadmap to Owning More, Working Less, and Creating the Life You Want*, by Mark Dolfini, The Landlord Coach

About the Author

Christine Luken, Founder of the Financial Dignity® Movement, is a Certified Divorce Specialist and Financial Counselor with more than 14 years of experience empowering others to master the emotional side of money. She is the author of *Money Is Emotional: Prevent Your Heart from Hijacking Your Wallet* and *Manage Money Like a Boss: A Financial Guide for Creative Entrepreneurs.*

Acknowledgments

H ere are the many people on my book launch team who deserve a great big Thank You.

Almighty God, thank you for the breath in my lungs and the fire in my words. May your light continue to shine through me into the financial darkness of others.

My Mom (Carol Mitchell), thank you for always being my biggest encourager and closest confidant.

My Dad (Tom Luzak), thank you for always believing in me and being proud of me, no matter what.

Nicholle Bays, my best and dearest soul friend, thank you for being my constant companion on this journey called life. You're one of the few who's truly seen my before and after, and loved me through it all.

My amazing friend, Heather, and owner of Red Golden Publishing, thank you for creating my stunning cover design and guidance on marketing this book. You make the package as amazing as the contents. I want to publish every future book with you right by my side!

Gwenette Gaddis, my editor, thank you for polishing the rough edges off this gem to really make it shine.

Dan Bisig, Allison Dagney, and Jenny Cochran (my alpha readers), thank you! You've made this book better with your invaluable input and suggestions!

My "Dream Team," thank you for helping to spread the buzz about this book far and wide. I appreciate you!

My coaching clients, thank you for allowing me to be a part of your journey to lasting Financial Dignity®. I am honored and humbled that you trust me enough to let me into your vulnerable places so I can help you heal your relationship with money.

Finally, a big THANK YOU to all of my family, friends, and followers who supported me in some form or fashion during the writing of this book! There are far too many of you to mention by name; in fact, it would fill another book. Please know that I am eternally grateful for your love and support!

www.ingramcontent.com/pod-product-compliance
Lightning Source LLC
Chambersburg PA
CBHW020154090426
42734CB00008B/823